D0172302

Preface

In substance, though in much abbreviated form, the contents of this book were presented in April 1986 as the Schaff Lectures at Pittsburgh Theological Seminary, the Donnell Lectures at the Theological Seminary of the University of Dubuque, Iowa, and a minicourse of the Studies in Religion Program at the University of Michigan in Ann Arbor. To all who made the lectures possible and extended a warm welcome to my wife and me, I express my deep gratitude.

The Neukirchener Verlag, in D-4133 Neukirchen-Vluyn, has published in 1987 a much longer version under the title *Das Mahl des Herrn*. The German edition contains among other things the detailed references and arguments that could not be included in the American version and that may be sorely missed by researchers.

The Epilogue, which is devoted to the Lima papers ("BEM") of 1982, will make sense only when read after the four exegetical chapters. The Lima critique has been translated from the German by Lloyd Gaston, of Vancouver, British Columbia, and was first published in January 1986 by *Theology Today*, in Princeton.

It is my sincere hope that this book will contribute to reducing outdated and divisive disputes over the table to which Jesus Christ invites sinners such as we are.

Markus Barth
Riehen, near Basel, Switzerland

Contents

Rediscovering
The Lord's Supper

Communion with Israel,
with Christ,
and Among the Guests

Markus Barth

John Knox Press
ATLANTA

Acknowledgment is made to *Theology Today* for permission to reprint "BEM: Questions and Considerations," *Theology Today* (January 1986).

Library of Congress Cataloging-in-Publication Data

Barth, Markus.
  Rediscovering the Lord's Supper.

  Translation of: Das Mahl des Herrn.
  Includes index.
  1. Lord's Supper—Biblical teaching. 2. Bible.
N.T.—Criticism, interpretation, etc. I. Title.
BV823.B36313   1988   234'.163   87-46294
ISBN 0-8042-3749-2

Introduction

The Lord's Supper, whether it be called the mass, the mystery, the eucharist, or the communion, is something good and great, simple and deep, moving and practical. It is Christ who invites to his table; we are guests of the Crucified, who has promised to come again.

But what have we made of this invitation and the meal? I will mention only four examples to show how the very best has been exposed to corruption.

Very often the meal is overshadowed by a somber and depressing mood. The horrible death of Christ and the burden of personal and worldwide misery and sin make the guests of the Lord tremble. True enough, they take comfort in being accepted by Christ, and they enjoy receiving forgiveness and being dismissed in peace. Yet often the impression is created that it is only individual salvation and personal satisfaction that are sought, communicated, and actually experienced. This salvation and satisfaction are so much restricted to the soul or to a life after death that little or no attention is paid to the body, to the present plight and needs of human society, especially to the people who exist in appalling poverty, and to the many suffering creatures all over the world.

When and where is the communion meal still an act and example of mutual sharing, caring, and love? Is joy ever expressed in the presence of diverse, perhaps even strange and burdened participants? It looks as if religious self-concern and egotism have gained the upper hand. This contradicts the essence of the meal. How different is the role of the eucharist in the so-called base communities in Central and South America. There, the inclusion and the participation, the survival and the dignity of the poorest among the poor become the radiating core, and they shape the form of the meal.

A language has been fabricated for describing the mystery of the Lord's Supper, a language that is certainly learned, deep, mysterious, but hardly very clear and persuasive. The Bible itself does not speak of *sacrament, transubstantiation, consubstantiation, transfunctionalization, transsignification,* or *symbol* (a sign that shows what it effects and effects what it shows). Certainly the speech of *sub una, sub utraque,* or about concomitancy is not well known. The Supper has been wrapped in a smokescreen of very difficult language.

The cumbersome language has to do with the strange and curious questions that have been asked about the Lord's Supper. One who asks a wrong question is most likely to get a wrong answer. In discussion about the Lord's Supper, attention has been focused upon the interrelationship of spirit and matter, eternity and time, visible and invisible; and concepts such as effective sign have been created to bridge the gap. The question whether these philosophical questions are really at the heart of what the Bible tells us about the Lord's Supper, however, seems not to have been sufficiently pondered. Theologically unschooled people can hardly understand what scholars discuss, either boringly or passionately, among themselves. Some of their disputes concerning the Lord's Supper are so ambiguous and baffling that they do not really relate to the life and the needs of a congregation. Should it really be impossible to go beyond the traditional language and to bridge the communication gap so that everybody can understand and enjoy what biblical scholars and dogmatic thinkers are talking about?

It is a public scandal that many Christian communities exploit the doctrine and the celebration of the communion as a means of excommunication. This scandal persists, even though brave and risky steps are taken by pastors and priests, by student groups and scholars, by deacons and so-called laypeople, to redress this situation in several countries, especially in the framework of local congregations. But how often the function of the eucharist is and has been almost as divisive as the various concepts of the ministry, including the Vatican position concerning the papacy.

Something other than the unquestionable diversity or pluralism of the biblical pronouncements on the Holy Meal has caused fateful and obnoxious splits. The influx of Greek dualistic philosophy, the conscious or unconscious adoption of elements of the ancient mystery religions, and accommodations to Roman legal thought and political institutions are found at the root of the divisions. The contrast between spirit and matter, clergy and laity, holy and profane, religious experience and daily conduct, also the varieties of meanings inherent in the term *symbol* and the power ascribed to correctly pronounced formulas—such things have overlaid or even replaced the substance and the intentions of the biblical utterances of the Lord's Supper. In the Bible the thanksgiving addressed to God, the love among brothers and sisters, and the common witness to reconciliation and peace for all the world matter more than other concerns.

Historical-critical scholarship can and should provide help to get us out of the impasse in which we find ourselves when we celebrate the Lord's Supper and talk about it in Bible study groups. A careful study of what the Lord's Supper was originally meant to be and what after diverse developments has become of it may contribute to the search for unity among divided churches. On the other hand, that unity has sometimes been sought less in faithfulness to the Bible than in cheap compromises between liturgies and doctrines. To be sure, at meetings and in the publications of Roman Catholic, Eastern Orthodox, Protestant, and Free Church biblical experts, an amazing unity is sometimes experienced. In rare cases it includes the readiness to see and admit time-sanctioned errors and abuses. The following are among the so-called results of today's scholarly endeavors.

(1) The oldest form of the Lord's Supper is not known. Neither the Pauline and/or Lukan, nor the Markan and/or Matthean records of Jesus' last meal provide unambiguous evidence. Therefore, no one can claim to possess the original liturgy, interpretation, and application of the Supper.

(2) The Passover framework of the institution of the Lord's Supper, of which Mark, Matthew, and Luke emphatically and unanimously speak, is historically dubious and theologically irrelevant.

(3) Jesus' saying concerning the cup is considered a later addition made by the early church. The only authentic comment is the state-

ment on the bread for which Jesus gives thanks to God, and which he breaks and distributes.

(4) Some ancient manuscripts of Luke's Gospel contain neither the words "broken for you" nor Jesus' reference to the blood poured out for the making of the new covenant; the blood is not even mentioned. The so-called Short Luke ends, e.g., as the RSV of 1948 shows, with the word *bread* in Luke 22:19, omitting verse 20. Thus, no explicit emphasis is laid upon the sacrificial character of Jesus' death or upon the shedding of his blood. Instead, the shorter Lukan text, as well as the otherwise lengthy total account of Jesus' last meal (see Luke 22:14–38), harmonizes beautifully with the records of the foot washing and the discourses, which in John's Gospel are the highlights of Jesus' final supper with his disciples. In Luke 22:14–38; John 13:1–20; and also in John 13:21—17:26, community, humility, mutual service, and mission bear the main accents. However, probably a majority of historical-critical exegetes reject the priority and possible authenticity of the shorter Luke. It is believed that an excision has taken place during the transmission of Luke's institution account.

(5) Agreement is increasing between Catholics and Protestants that the substances of bread and wine are not being changed during the ceremony. The doctrine of physical transubstantiation is considered a serious and pious addition to the original, historical, and theological sense of the eucharistic texts of the Bible. There is no longer a minimal consensus between Lutherans and Roman Catholics that a careful, literal interpretation, using the modern tools of exegesis, must lead to the conclusion that the New Testament teaches transubstantiation or at least consubstantiation, that is, a new composition of the elements consumed by those participating in the meal.

(6) It is commonly accepted that the passages in the New Testament that describe Jesus Christ's last meal are not the only biblical basis, source, and criterion for properly understanding and celebrating the Lord's Supper. Almost equal importance is now attributed to the stories and sayings about Jesus' table communion, with both sinners and Pharisees; to the feeding of the thousands by Jesus; to the parables concerning meals and the role of meals within some parables; to the table communion Christ shared with his disciples after his resurrection (the so-called Easter meals); and to the promises concerning a heavenly table and the joys to be found in Abraham's lap.

(7) Finally, though it is by no means denied that the Lord's Supper as depicted in the New Testament has ethical implications (for a life of service, love, and mission), scholars are shying away from describing the essence, sense, and function of the Lord's Supper as "only ethical."

Some of these exegetical agreements contain serious suggestions. However, not all of them prevent doubt, nor do they forbid further inquiries and debates. Several of them have so far contributed nothing to a joyful rediscovery and celebration of the meal. The reasons for a cordial disagreement with some of them will be shown in the chapters that follow. All the arguments I have mentioned attempt, in substance and in form, to interpret the main eucharistic texts of the New Testament. A new attempt to interpret even these texts shall be made.

This is not to claim that only exegetical questions call for discussion. Dogmatic, liturgical, ethical, sociological, and psychological research must complement the approach I use here. But Bible study is necessary whenever a church is open to being reformed by God's word and to rediscovering the meal instituted by Jesus Christ.

Chapter 1 is a discussion of the relationship between the Passover and the Lord's Supper, as revealed by the first three (so-called Synoptic) Gospels. In chapter 2 the focus is upon the community with Christ, about which the Apostle Paul speaks in 1 Corinthians 10. In chapter 3 the community among Christ's guests comes into view as it is dramatically unfolded in 1 Corinthians 11 and in Luke's writings. Finally, in chapter 4 the specific witness of John 6 and the term *sacrament* is discussed at some length.

1

Communion with Israel

Learning from the Passover How to Celebrate the Lord's Supper and Learning from the Jews How to Serve God

Whether we like to be reminded of it or not, all Christian churches owe a debt of gratitude to the Jews. From them we have taken over, for example: (1) the vocabulary and concepts used in speaking of God and of humankind; (2) the main part of the Bible, the so-called Old Testament; (3) the psalms we sing and many of the prayers we pray; (4) the assembly on the seventh day for worship; (5) the central position of the Word of God in a worship that does not include bloody sacrifices. The bond is especially close when the Passover and the Lord's Supper are compared. Within a traditional Jewish Passover celebration, according to the first three Gospels, Jesus Christ instituted the Lord's Supper.

The Way of the Passover

To answer the question what was and what is the Passover (Seder), I rely upon two main sources of information: invitations from American Jews, between 1960 and 1972, to participate in Seder celebrations held in Jewish homes and in Conservative and Reform synagogues; and the study of scholarly and other literature, mostly of Jewish origin, ranging from the books of the Law, the Prophets, and the Psalms to the Mishna Tractate Pesahim and to modern liturgies and learned treatments of the Passover.

One result of my participation and study is the realization that it would be precocious to speak of "the Jewish Passover." The Passover is a way of worship on which the Jewish people have moved during their history of more than three thousand years. It is not a timeless principle, prescription, or doctrine that excludes growth, development, and an eventual completion.

According to the book of Exodus (chs. 12—13) it is likely that two originally separate festivals (one for shepherds and one for farmers, both of which may have been called Passover) existed before the Israelites began to celebrate their own feast. Exodus 12:11 and 12:27 speak distinctly of the specific Passover *of the Lord*, which henceforth is to be celebrated. The Passover of the Lord combines the celebration of farmers, who bring and eat before their God fresh bread prepared from the yield of their fields, and the celebration of shepherds, who offer their lambs. Obviously, the first biblical reports imply that the cowboy and the farmer should be friends; they are to unite their gifts in a spring festival. For both of them, this festival receives a new meaning: Israel's festival, that is, the Lord's Passover, transcends a celebration in honor of nature and of the productivity of human labor. At its center no longer stand periodical events such as the cycle of the four seasons, the coming and going of cold and warm weather, of dry and wet seasons, of hunger and thirst, and of eating and drinking. Now God's unique interference is solemnly "remembered": the liberation of farmers and shepherds and a whole people from captivity and slavery in Egypt. The Hebrew word *pasach* (from which *Pesach, Passa,* and *Passover* are derived) no longer describes a (limping?) dance ritual performed by the people, but the passing-by of the Lord or the angel of destruction who is about to smite the firstborn of the Egyptians (Exod. 12:13, 23, 27). In summary the festival has ceased to be a celebration of nature and has become the memorial of a glorious historical event. The month of redemption from Egypt became the first month of Israel's calendar. The original participants in the feast were in a hurry: they girded their loins with a belt, they wore sandals on their feet, and they carried walking staffs in their hands. The rush and the pressure are expressed by the unleavened bread that was (and is) to be consumed. They had no time to wait until fresh dough was leavened (Exod. 12:11, 34; Deut. 16:3).

After Israel left Egypt, in the wilderness years, at the foot of Mount Sinai, and in Kadesh, where Israel was camped for decades, the festival of the Passover was probably not celebrated; no evidence exists for these periods. According to the Bible, Joshua, Moses' successor as leader of Israel, reintroduced it only *after* Israel entered the promised land (Josh. 5:10).

Not even this restoration of the feast succeeded in making the Passover an annual ceremony. For 2 Chronicles 30 and 2 Kings 23 tell us that King Hezekiah, sometime before 700 B.C., or King Josiah, sometime after 622 B.C., reinstituted the rite, tearing it out of the oblivion and neglect into which it had fallen.

Still later, priestly festival calendars were composed, probably during and after the period of the Babylonian Exile rather than before it. In Leviticus 23:5–8; Numbers 9:2–4; 28:16–25; and Deuteronomy 16:1–8 (cf. Ezra 6:19–22), legal prescriptions say when and how to arrange the Passover sacrifice and meal. Details concerning the exact date, the use of the lamb and its blood, the use of the matzoth (pieces of unleavened bread), the festival assemblies to be held—all that is fixed in the later writings, though with some changes in comparison with the wording of Exodus 12—13.

The legalistic canonizations contain four specific accents. Numbers 28:16–25 prescribes manifold burnt offerings and the slaughtering of a goat, calling the latter a sin offering for atonement. So the Passover was moved into the series of atoning sacrifices. In Deuteronomy 16:1–8, all offerings are restricted, and even the eating of the Passover animal is limited, to one location: to Jerusalem, the place and sanctuary chosen by God. Until the rediscovery of the so-called Deuteronomy, the code of law found in a temple-wall, the Passover animal could be slaughtered and eaten in any Jewish community. When the Passover sacrifice was centralized, the blood was to be poured out at the foot of the altar on which the animal had been slaughtered. Ezekiel 45:19–23 takes up an apparently neglected element of the original Passover night, saying that the blood was to be painted on the doorposts of the temple. Together with all other sacrifices, Ezekiel definitely treats the Passover as a sin offering for forgiveness. Eventually, the Passover blood received the same dignity as the drops of blood that flow at the circumcision ceremony. According to the Talmud, some rabbis spoke of two bloods of atonement— one the circumcision blood, the other the blood of the Passover. In Exodus 12:43, the Passover was reserved for Jews, even for those circumcised according to the Mosaic prescription. But circumcised servants or slaves living in Jewish households were entitled to participate in the festival meal (Exod. 12:43–49).

During the hellenistic period, the mode of celebration moved even further away from the great hurry prescribed in Exodus 12:11. After the time of Emperor Alexander, when his successors had divided his empire among themselves, the Israelites met in festival rooms. Beginning in about 300 or 250 B.C. the rooms were furnished with couches, as if the celebration were meant to be the equivalent of a Greek festival meal, a so-called symposium. At this time (if not earlier) wine was added to the elements that were consumed during the celebration, though the apocryphal book of Jubilees, which was written about 125 B.C., dates the use of wine to the night of the Exodus. Toward the end of the meal, so the rabbinic Mishna (composed in written form during the second century after Christ but containing evidence from the time of Christ) presupposes, some of the participants found for themselves a place under, rather than at, the table. In the Mishna the term *sleeping* is a euphemism, a kind way of denoting serious lack of full consciousness. Obviously drunkenness at the festival table, as castigated by Paul in 1 Corinthians 11:21, was occurring not only when pagans met to carouse in their homes or temples. Jews, too, could feel so overhappy with the freedom granted to them by God (foreign occupation troops in their homeland notwithstanding) that some of them drank more than necessary.

When Jesus held his last meal with his disciples, the Passover meal, he had an opportunity to call for some drastic reforms. He might have protested against the use of couches, of pillows, or of upholstered chairs because they contradicted the haste of God's migrating people on the night of the Exodus. He might have objected to the use of wine the night before his death because it implied the risk (which is depicted as drastic reality in the musical *Jesus Christ Superstar*) that some would get drunk. He might have initiated a reform that would have led to a celebration more like that of Israel's ancestors. Had he done so, he would certainly have dampened the joy that was customary to the Passover celebration of his time. But he did none of these. Rather, he told his disciples to prepare the supper in an upper room having couches; he gave them ample time not only to buy the lamb and have it slaughtered but also to procure the additional ingredients for the meal. And they had to look for the wine!

In later periods, further additions and changes occurred. Three examples deserve mention.

The role of children during the meal has grown more and more important. According to today's Passover liturgies, one child (Exod. 13:8, 14), or several children (Exod. 12:26), have to ask questions such as "What do you mean by this service?" "Why is this night different from all other nights?" A firm liturgical order has emerged: the first three of four children ask sensible questions in a pious tone, and each of them receives a suitable, kind, and happy answer. However, the fourth child has to play the part of an atheist, an agnostic, or a skeptic. More or less openly the fourth child expresses the opinion, if not conviction, that the whole feast is utter nonsense. This child is given a clear and sharp answer, e.g., "If all of us were thinking as you are, we would still be slaves in Egypt." The strong rebuke does not obliterate the astonishing fact that a representative of atheism or skepticism is included in the liturgy and makes a contribution to the festival. The idea that such a person ought to be kept away from the common table, even excommunicated, is clearly replaced by pedagogic wisdom and a sense of liturgical drama. More is achieved this way than by official condemnation and the self-righteous slamming of doors.

Comfortable seats have been retained since the first century, and wine is always offered. At least four cups are prescribed for each participant. Before the meal, arrangements are made for a very careful search of the Jewish houses; all vestiges of leavened food have to be found and removed. It is fun for the father and the children to go hunting for impure stuff under beds and carpets, behind wardrobes.

At a Jewish celebration one great chair catches special attention. It

is gloriously outfitted, and a huge cup filled with wine stands ready for
its occupant. The chair is set up for Elijah, for this prophet a cup is
filled to the brim. Often windows and doors are left open so that the
messenger of the end time, the forerunner of the Messiah, knows that
he is expected and welcome. It is as essential today as it was in earlier
forms of the memorial feast that the celebration is not complete in
itself. It stretches its arms toward the future; the hope for something
even better to come rules the day. Those assembled hope and pray and
yearn for the great liberation and the final gathering of all Jewish
people in the rebuilt city of Jerusalem.

Sometimes non-Jewish persons are invited to the celebration—and
not for playing the role of the oppressive Egyptians. Among the many
liturgies used, some make it unmistakably clear that the memorial of
the liberation of the Jews is also an expression of trust in the promise
that one day God will grant freedom to all nations and each one of
their members. Everyone will be free from oppression, exploitation,
hunger, segregation, and all other forms of unrighteousness.

Essential Features of the Passover

The historical survey of the Passover given so far can be supple-
mented by listing some of the elements common to the Passover liturgies during diverse periods.

(1) The celebration takes place in memory of, or as a memorial to,
a unique, complete, and perfect act of God: the Exodus from Egypt in
the thirteenth century b.c. (Exod. 12:14; 13:3, 8—10, 14—16; Deut.
16:3). Two meanings of *remembrance* are, in Western languages, very
far, even excluded, from the Hebrew senses of this word. The first is
the notion that remembrance means no more than an intellectual or
emotional recollection of an ancient tale or event. A proper rendition
of the biblical word is *celebration*, that is, a public, common,
dramatic, and festival expression of joy and gratitude for what God
has done. Soul and body, the ear, the mouth, the stomach, the
sentiments and actions, of the participants are involved. Briefly,
remembrance is an action of the faithful, an action destined to the
praise and glory of a great deed by God.

Equally excluded is the idea that by remembrance, God's basic
action is repeated, put into effect, validated, actualized, or applied—
as if God's action were in need of, and in some sense dependent on, a

religious ceremony. True enough, in pagan religious thought and practice an intimate connection exists between myth and ritual. The relevance of the timeless tale, which is sometimes compressed into sacred formulas, becomes concrete and effective, confirmed and validated only by the reenactment of the "holy word" in cultic form. The role of the Marduk myth in the neo-Babylonian Akitu festival is an example. Mircea Eliade has convincingly elaborated on the transposition of the mythical *illo tempore* to the needs of the *hic et nunc*. Only when the timeless tales and symbols are re-presented by cultic reenactment do they become relevant and saving for the celebrating community and valid for the whole current generation.

The myth-ritual syndrome does not apply to the biblical Jewish Passover festival. The redemption from Egypt is an event in history, not a timeless myth. In history God has revealed who God is, not just what God may be, provided cultic personnel use the proper formulas and complete prescribed actions in front of a believing community. The history created by God is exemplary: it gives confidence that the solutions to the problems of the present are in God's hand and that God's great action in the past includes the promise of a bright future. But the gratitude for God's completed act and for its implications for present and coming days does not mean that God's act and the repeated human cultic action are identified with each other. Some biblical texts state this explicitly: "he . . . spared *our* houses [emphasis added]" (Exod. 12:27); "when *I* came out of Egypt [in that night, not only now, in this Passover celebration] . . . . by strength of hand the LORD brought *us* out of Egypt [emphasis added]" the Passover celebrants confess (Exod. 13:8, 14, 16; cf. Deut. 26:7–9: "Then we cried to the LORD, the God of our Fathers . . . and the LORD brought *us* out of Egypt [emphasis mine]"). The Mishna (Pesahim X.5) sums this up beautifully: "Each [Israelite] shall celebrate as one who has gone out of Egypt." (The version "as though he had gone out" is misleading because it denies that through their ancestors all Jews have already been led out of captivity.) God's perfect act is recited and confessed in the Passover rather than reenacted or made valid and real only in the cultic ceremony. The celebration is a sign on the hand and a mark on the forehead of each Israelite (Exod. 13:9, 16). Although it is a memorial and festival of liberation, it is not in itself a redemptive event.

(2) The words "this is," which are found in the institution texts of

the eucharist, have a precedent in the Passover liturgy. As mentioned, the children or the son of the house asks, "What do you mean by this service?" or "Why are we doing this?" To such questions the answer is given, "It is the sacrifice of the LORD's Passover, for he passed over the houses of the people of Israel in Egypt . . . [and] spared our houses. . . . It is because of what the LORD did for me when I came out of Egypt. . . . the LORD brought us out of Egypt" (Exod. 12:26–27; 13:8, 14, 16). Although special food (that is, unleavened bread) is eaten on the seven festival days prescribed for the feast, the responses to the questions describe *why* the whole festival takes place. The question "What do we eat?" or "What is the substance of the bread and wine?" has not been asked and is not answered.

(3) Before the destruction of the second temple and the cessation of bloody sacrifices in A.D. 70, the slaughtering of the sacrificial animals was *one* liturgical element of the Passover celebration. Another was the drinking of wine and the eating of the meat and the herbs, spices, and sauces that are a part of the meal. The eating and the drinking were a consequence, not a part, of the sacrifice itself. According to the Old Testament, several sacrifices were connected with a sacrificial meal, which followed the bloody ritual. Sacrifice and sacrificial meal must not be equated. An altar was necessary for the first, a table for the second. Of the blood "poured out" during the slaughtering, nothing was carried to the table. That blood should be drunk from the cup is an impossible idea! Even what happens today in and through the Passover celebrations in Jewish communities is certainly not a bloodless reenactment of the sacrifice; neither is it a repetition of the Exodus. It is an offering of thanksgiving, which the psalms call *toda*, a public praise of the Lord for liberation from death, disease, captivity, loneliness. Indeed, since the time of Deuteronomy, the Passover lamb had to be slaughtered in the presence of a priest at the temple. However, the meal held in the houses did not depend upon the presence of an ordained person.

(4) The feast, service, ordinance, or memorial of which the Old Testament Passover texts speak (see, e.g., Exod. 12:14, 17, 24–25; 13:10) is a communal affair and cannot be celebrated either in private or simply for personal benefit. Certainly the reality of the worshipers' personal sin and guilt, on the one hand, and of gracious atonement and

forgiveness by God, on the other, were eventually included in the teaching about the Passover. Along with the political, social, juridical deliverance from Egypt, the deliverance from sin (cf. Pss. 103:3–4; 130:8) became more and more a reason for celebrating. However, the individual Israelite, with personal needs and hopes, has never been the end of God's ways; rather, individual salvation and hope have always been included in the marvelous things God has done and is still expected to do for the whole chosen people.

It has pleased God to maintain and carry the people Israel not only by the sending of prophets and wise persons but also—as, for example, Herman Wouk has shown—by the ever repeated ceremonies. They have been used by God to keep the people alive and together, even in the dispersion and after the destruction of Jerusalem, when such central institutions and symbols as the temple and the sacrifices no longer existed.

The Lord's Supper in the Light of the Passover

Whether modern scholars like it or not, all three of the Synoptic Gospels affirm that Jesus' last meal was a Passover meal. This meal was held on the evening after the room selected for that purpose had been cleaned, the couches for the guests arranged, the vegetables and other ingredients of the supper bought, and the lamb slaughtered and prepared for the table. According to Luke (22:15) Jesus opened the meal in a very emotional tone: "I have ardently longed [literally, 'with great desire I have desired'] to eat this Passover with you before I suffer." The Synoptic embedding of the institution of the Lord's Supper in the Passover framework defies neglect by scholarly interpreters. Certainly Paul and the Gospel of John do not explicitly establish, confirm, or expound this connection. But even they do not discuss Jesus the Bread of Life without reference to Israel's history. The gift of manna is mentioned in 1 Corinthians 10:1–13 and in John 6:31–32, 49, 53. The sacrificial meal, which Israel's priests were privileged to receive from the altar, is drawn into Paul's argument for comparison in 1 Corinthians 9:13; 10:18. All references to *remembrance, blood of the covenant poured out* (for forgiveness of sin), *new covenant,* as well as the phrases *for you* and *for many,* carry the connotations they bear in Israel's Bible and worship. All Old Testament quotes and allusions found in the New Testament underline the bond between Israel and the church. This is true even when tensions and contrasts become apparent, as in, e.g., Galatians 3—4 and 2 Corinthians 3.

For an understanding of how the references to the Passover bear upon one's comprehension of the institution and meaning of the Lord's Supper, observations such as the following may be decisive.

As already observed, the words *this is* (at the beginning of the words spoken over the bread and the cup) do not respond to the question, "What are we eating and drinking now?" In fact, the controversial word *is* (Latin *est*) was not part of the Aramaic (or Hebrew?) diction used by Jesus. The question presupposed by Jesus' words over the bread and the cup is "Why are we celebrating this meal?" This may be the reason that in the Greek text Jesus begins the the sentence spoken over the bread with the neuter pronoun *this* (*touto*), not the masculine (*houtos*), which might have clearly restricted Jesus' words to a comment on the bread and its substance.

Sacrificial flesh and blood poured out did belong to the Passover celebration. Approximately 10,000 lambs were slaughtered annually for the Passover groups assembling in Jerusalem. Then Jesus announced that *his* body and *his* blood were replacing the function formerly fulfilled by the meat and by the blood of the Passover lamb. *My* body and *my* blood—"this is" what henceforth forms the basis of communal celebration. Though he may be compared to a lamb (Jer. 11:19; Isa. 53:7), Jesus is not *a* lamb that is slaughtered for the benefit of Israelites only. Rather, he is "the lamb of God that carries away the sin of the world" (John 1:29, 36; cf. 1 Peter 1:19; Rev. 5:6, 9, 12). To use Paul's words, "As our Passover Lamb, Christ has been slaughtered" (1 Cor. 5:7, author's translation). The epistle to the Hebrews does not mention the Passover but uses the Yom Kippur to illustrate the uniqueness of Jesus Christ's *one* great sacrifice, which was made for all the sins ever committed and which is distinct from the many daily sacrifices offered at the Jewish temple. Jesus Christ's death crowns, and at the same time contrasts with, all other sacrifices. Therefore, at the Lord's table the words "This is . . ." are the beginning of a statement about why his disciples are to continue meeting at his table, not about the substance of the food.

Only under one condition can the words *"this is"* be understood either to indicate or to reveal *and* to effect transubstantiation, consubstantiation, a symbolic function, a transfunctionalization, transsignification, or similar changes that seem mutually exclusive and that have separated churches from one another. The condition exists when interpreters despise or ignore the Passover framework in which the Synoptic writers embedded their accounts of the institution of the Lord's Supper. If, however, this setting is taken seriously (i.e., if the Passover framework is not considered theologically irrelevant), Jesus' words about the bread and the cup mean that it is Christ, Christ alone, who brings the final sacrifice, which is acceptable to God. It is Christ alone who is the mediator of the new covenant—the covenant that includes the Gentiles. Therefore, his words over the bread and the cup describe himself, not a mysterious change that is taking place in the bread and wine. When he says, "Do this in *my* remembrance"—the word *my* is accentuated in the Greek text—he does not speak of the remembrance of a continuous ever-new miracle that he will perform on physical elements. Jesus asks for faith in himself and for faithfulness to himself alone; he is not calling for belief in a physical or spiritual change or a transformation of bread and wine.

During the meal Jesus refers to his *body* and his *blood*. In this context, *body* probably has the same meaning as *flesh*. Indeed, in John 6:51–56 reference is made to Christ's flesh and blood rather than to his body and blood, and in Hebrews 2:14 mention is made of his blood and his flesh. The reason for the exchangeability of the two words *flesh* and *body* may well be this: Jesus used the Aramaic word *guf* (or *gupa*), which can be translated either *flesh* or *body*. Similarly, in Pauline diction *body* and *flesh* are sometimes used as synonyms (e.g., in 1 Cor. 6:16; Eph. 5:28–31). It is necessary, though, to distinguish between two meanings of *body and blood* or *flesh and blood*.

The words *flesh and blood* are used in one breath in statements such as "Flesh and blood has not revealed this to you" (Matt. 16:17); "I did not confer with flesh and blood" (Gal. 1:16); "flesh and blood cannot inherit the kingdom of God" (1 Cor. 15:50). In these instances the nouns form a unit denoting humankind, human nature, humanity. Even without the addition of *and blood*, *flesh* or *body* can describe a person; *my body* can mean simply "my self," or "I," (Eph. 5:28; cf. Rom. 12:1) much as *my soul* in some psalms (e.g., Ps. 103:1) means "myself."

During his last meal, Jesus "gives" bread and the cup to the disciples, and he interprets these actions by speaking of his body's being *given* or *broken* (as various readings of Luke 22:19 and 1 Cor. 11:24 have it) and of his blood being poured out. From the meaning of *body* (flesh) *and blood* just described, a grave conclusion has been drawn (most eloquently, e.g., by Eduard Schweizer) in almost all (except the Zwinglian) interpretations of the institution texts. They assume that during the last meal and henceforth during the Lord's Supper, Jesus "gives himself" to those sitting at his table. In giving bread and wine, Jesus then actually gives himself to the disciples. The two gifts—the physical and the personal (spiritual) presents—would in this case not only be given simultaneously but would be inseparably combined by Jesus Christ's will, words, and perpetual institution.

I stated earlier that the Lord's Supper is certainly much more than an act of intellectual and/or emotional remembrance performed by the disciples who were called to "do this." But does Christ really give himself at his table? The Supper would have a *sacramental* sense and power if at the table Christ were both the giver and the gift of a bread that is entirely different from the physical bread that is on other occasions blessed, broken, given, and eaten. The same pertains to the wine in the cup. Then, in, with, under, or through the earthly substances of bread and wine, Christ would hand out himself. If this were true, he would be as much and as truly *in* the bread and *in* the wine as the divine Logos was present in the womb of the Virgin Mary, in Jesus walking the streets of Galilee and Jerusalem, and as the eternal Son of God was present in the body hanging on the cross and in his appearances after the resurrection. Bold interpreters speak of a continuation or an extension of the incarnation. John 6:32–58 (which is discussed in ch. 4) seems to support and prove true even this interpretation. The Last Supper is then a means of grace because in this meal, in a unique way that is necessary for all who believe in him and want to have a share in him, he is the giver *and* the gift.

Certainly, this widespread, high sacramental understanding ignores the framework of the Passover meal. Actually it negates it, for it makes obsolete all elements of remembrance and celebration that may tie the church to Israel. The church's separation from Israel might have to be accepted as an unalterable fact if it were not based on at least three problematic assumptions.

According to the first assumption, that which is given is physical bread and the person of Christ at the same time. This assumption is questionable because at least two modes of giving and two gifts are distinguished in the New Testament. One meaning is the repeated solemn distribution of bread, which is described in the stories of Christ feeding the thousands and of Christ breaking bread during his last meal and in the house near Emmaus. Then and there Christ was present and active in person, and he handed out bread. Still he was simultaneously present in another form, that is, in the bread. Or else he would on several occasions before and after his death have distributed—and consumed—nothing less than himself in the form of bread! The other meaning of *giving* is found in statements such as "God so loved the world that he gave his only son" and "Jesus loved us and gave himself for us" (John 3:16; Gal. 2:20; Eph. 5:2, 25; cf. John 6:51). This unique, unrepeatable, once-for-all, glorious, and valid gift is the substance of the statement in the institution texts, "This is my body given [or broken] for you." If instead of *for you*, we read *to you*, the simultaneity of the gift of bread and of Jesus' own self-giving might be indicated. However, the words *for you* (or *for us* or *for me* or *for many*) always speak of the event that took place on the cross.

Second, John 6 has been combined with the institution texts, and the interpretation of these texts has been based mainly, even exclusively, on this chapter. This combination has been customary from the days of the second-century church, through the Middle Ages, to the Lutheran and Calvinist Reformations and many modern interpretations. It constitutes a grave and risky exegetical step. For it is hardly very scholarly to disregard the distinct witness and diction of the fourth Gospel and to ignore the fact that in John's description of Jesus' last meal (ch. 13) the foot washing stands in the center and the speech on the bread of life is found in the entirely different and far removed context of John 6.

The third presupposition of the sacramentalistic interpretation consists of neglecting or ignoring an important fact. The terms *body* (flesh) and *blood* often have a meaning that is different from the one unfolded so far; they denote not only "humanity," "human nature," but something more.

Whenever the words *flesh* and *blood* appear in separate, though often successive, statements in the Bible, they refer to a killing—be it on a hunt, by murder, or during a sacrifice performed by a priest. The texts sometimes speak of blood that is *poured out, shed*. During his last meal, Christ made separate statements over the bread and the cup, and he made these statements in independent sentences. His blood is—except in the text of 1 Corinthians 11:25—called "poured-out" blood. And reference is made to his body (in Paul) or to his blood (in Matthew and Mark) or to both (in Luke) as being given "for you" or "for many."

The second sense of *body and blood* calls for the following interpretation of the institution texts: in the celebration of a Jewish sacrificial meal, even the Passover, Jesus announces and predicts that he will die, because he will be "given" away by God and will give himself unto death, i.e., his blood will be "shed." This giving and shedding will take place on the cross. Later, after Christ's death and resurrection, the apostles, evangelists, and teachers will proclaim the death of the Lord. Christ crucified will be the heart of their message (1 Cor. 1:18; 2:2). Then the congregation at the Lord's table will join in this confession, proclaiming "the Lord's death" (1 Cor. 11:26). During his last meal, Jesus himself reveals his priestly function and the sacrificial character of his death. Then and there, he proclaims his imminent death in such a manner that it cannot be misunderstood as merely a sad accident or a crime or a stroke of blind fate. Much more, his death is designated as a sacrifice offered *for* the benefit of others.

Sacrifice is no longer a term that is generally cherished in learned theological or more popular church parlance. Either it is all too heavily burdened with pagan ideas of paying, bribing, influencing a deity, or it belongs in patriotic speeches about the victims of a war, or its sense is cheapened so that it means no more than the "offering of" a financial contribution. How often sacrifice is understood to denote no more than a human work and performance, in religious context a movement from our side toward the deity by which the divine power will somehow be so changed that it will act in favor of the worshiper!

In the Bible, however, the words used for sacrifice have another, deep, beautiful, and indispensable sense and function. Almost always, unlike the meaning in nonbiblical cultic and secular texts, in the majority of the historical, doctrinal, liturgical, and legal biblical passages of the Old and New Testaments, *sacrifice* is an act, a gift, a revelation made by God toward us. In the words "God so loved the world that he gave his only Son" (John 3:16), the sacrifice meant is that which God brought for the benefit of all creatures. Clearly, God's gift to us, not our gift to God, is described. God's gift consists of the creation, mission, institution, of a priestly person who intercedes before God on behalf of a sinful people—as illustrated by Moses in Exodus 32:30–32, when he prays for the people who made the golden calf; by the servant of the Lord in Isaiah 53:12; and by the high priest on the Day of Atonement (Lev. 16). One of the functions of blood spilled by the priests was to make not only the human voice but also the blood cry out to God for intervention and help. This way Abel's blood cried from the soil, and the epistle to the Hebrews asserts that even louder and better does Christ's blood cry and intervene on our behalf (Gen. 4:10; Heb. 12:24). When a child is run over by a car, the blood poured out upon the street cries louder than any voice. Thus the blood of the sacrifice appeals to God to interfere and to manifest God's own righteousness toward us. According to the epistle to the Hebrews, Jesus Christ is the God-given priest and sacrifice because of the intercession he makes for us in his own death, his own blood. In Romans 3:24–26, Paul calls Christ the mediator (or the means) of atonement "brought forth" by God. According to Romans 8:34 and throughout Hebrews, he who has been raised and enthroned at God's side is making intercession on our behalf. The New Testament reports on Jesus' Last Supper, together with the passages containing Jesus' earlier predictions of his death and resurrection, are anticipated in the statement that his life is given "as a ransom for many" (Mark 10:45; Matt. 20:28). Therefore not only some latter-day theologians but Jesus himself, if we follow the New Testament evidence, called his death a sacrifice. Certainly Jesus' saying over the cup is more explicit about the sacrificial character of Jesus' death than is the comment made over the bread. But this is hardly a sufficient reason to dispute its historical authenticity.

To know that Christ's death was a sacrifice means to know that humankind—however guilt-laden, miserable, helpless—has been given one person who loves the people, dies *for* us, and intercedes eternally on our behalf at God's right hand.

In the Lord's Supper, Christ and his death are remembered as the one good cause for joy, hope, and gratitude. The eucharist is, even more than the Passover, a joyful festival—not in spite of, but because of, Christ's death. To celebrate the Lord's Supper in the mood of a funeral service or to try to transform it into an institution that has no higher purpose than to satisfy the religious needs of individuals surely contradicts the intention of the host at the Lord's table. Certainly, in Matthew's Gospel, "forgiveness of sins" is mentioned; the forgiveness of each person's fall and most miserable failures are in mind. Therefore, it is legitimate, maybe even necessary, to mention forgiveness or justification by grace alone at each celebration of the Lord's Supper. But the purpose and effect of Christ's death include more than personal forgiveness; otherwise it would be hard to explain why Mark, Luke, and Paul omit any mention of forgiveness and speak only of the covenant or the new covenant or the gift of Jesus' body or blood (or both) for us or for many. Indeed, in the New Testament, forgiveness is connected with, and shown to be dependent upon, Christ's death, upon his Word or his Spirit, and upon repentance and faith. Although this connection is essential and clearly attested to by many passages, only one of the four Supper institution texts makes it explicit—Matthew 26:28. In this text (unlike, e.g., Matt. 16:19; John 20:23) the Lord says nothing to indicate that the church or its officers have full power (or a monopoly) to handle, apply, or mediate forgiveness. In the eucharist, Jesus Christ alone is remembered—just as in the Passover, God alone is celebrated, not a mediating role of Israel, of Moses, or of divine worship. God liberated the people by a strong arm rather than by material, symbolic, and clerical assistance.

The institution texts of Luke and Paul speak of the *new covenant*. The cup-words in Matthew and Mark do not include the adjective *new*, but this omission hardly changes the meaning of the whole sentence. The reference to the new covenant should not be understood to emphasize exclusively the *difference* between the old and the new covenants, the Old and the New Testaments, or the supposedly old people and the so-called new people of God. By no means does the Lord's Supper signify, above all, a radical break between Israel and the church.

It may be objected that in Galatians 4:21–31 and 2 Corinthians 3, Paul uses strong words to compare and contrast the two covenants. Flesh and Spirit, letter and Spirit, servitude and freedom, death and life, condemnation and justification, a hiding veil and a glorious revelation—these are among the key terms with which Paul describes distinctions. Indeed it looks as if the new covenant were a totally different covenant and as if any positive relationship between the Passover meal and the Supper celebrated and instituted by Jesus were excluded—if not by Matthew and Luke, then certainly by the Apostle Paul.

However, the use of the term *new covenant* does not automatically demonstrate Jesus' intention to malign or abrogate the covenant that God made with Israel. When Paul extols the overarching glory of the new covenant, he also affirms the glory of the old (2 Cor. 3:7–11). After being thrown out of Abraham's household, Hagar and her son Ishmael, the allegorical representatives of the slavehood covenant, were sent back by God's angel and remained under God's protection and blessing (Gen. 16:7–16; 17:13, 18–20). These facts and others are all too easily forgotten when the term *new covenant* is given an anti-judaistic meaning, thus poisoning the term for Jews as well as for Christians, however welcomed by Marcion (an anti-Jewish heretic of the second century) and his early, later, and present-day followers.

The true meaning of the term *new covenant* must be derived from the statements that Hosea, Jeremiah, and Ezekiel make about the relationship between God, Israel, and Judah (Hos. 1—2; Jer. 2—3; 31:31–34; 33:20–26; Ezek. 16; 34; 36). God has chosen and loved Israel and made this people his wife; Jeremiah and Ezekiel go as far as to speak of two wives, the Northern Kingdom of Israel (Samaria) and the Southern Kingdom of Judah (Jerusalem). First, Israel turned away from the Lord and forsook her merciful and faithful husband. Then Judah did the same. By idolatry the female partner(s) of God broke the covenant. But what God's people do and what God does are not the same. When people break the covenant, that does not mean that God has broken it also. Only Jeremiah 3:8 avers that God has given

(Northern) Israel a letter of divorce and thereby annulled the marriage. But in God's name Hosea calls Israel to return to her husband, and other prophets invite the Northern and Southern sisters to repent and return to the Lord. They promise that God will *renew* the broken covenant in the end by uniting both nations into one people, by the gift of one king, the Holy Spirit, forgiveness, and a new heart. The renewed covenant is called "eternal." Therefore, according to the prophets mentioned, the new covenant is not another covenant with a different partner; it is the restitution and crowning of the original love and marriage relationship. By no means does God resemble a husband who for one reason or another divorces his wife and marries a young woman.

In Matthew's version of the cup-words (26:28), just as in Jeremiah 31:31–34 and elsewhere, covenant and forgiveness belong together. Indeed they are inseparable. In all institution reports of the Synoptic Gospels, the Passover framework indicates Jesus' positive attitude to the worship of Israel, even when—as elaborated in the epistle to the Hebrews (esp. 8:13)—the priesthood and the sacrifices of Israel are declared fulfilled and superseded by the one eternal Priest, Christ, and by the one eternally valid covenant, which has been established by the sacrificial death of Christ.

One other difference exists between the old and the renewed covenants. The Passover of the Jews, according to the biblical order, can be celebrated only by the people liberated from Egypt. Only by their circumcision can foreign-born people be included. The blood of the original Passover lamb protected only the houses and families of the Hebrews. According to Matthew and Mark, however, the blood of Jesus Christ is "poured out for many." The word *many* refers (as early as Isa. 53:11; cf. 52:15) not only to the sinners in Israel but also to the Gentile nations. When Luke and Paul say that the body or the body and the blood or the poured-out blood is given "for you" (i.e., so it seems, for a very limited group of people), then Luke, the author of the book of the Acts of the Apostles, and Paul, the exemplary missionary to the Gentiles, seem to restrict the benefit of Christ's death to Jewish-born disciples. Actually, these (weak and sinful) disciples represent the fulfillment of Israel's mission, not the retraction of God's promises, which have always pertained to both—the Jews and the nations. At all times, beginning with Abraham's calling, Israel was promised that its blessing was to be shared with and by all generations and nations. Israel was chosen to be a priestly people among and for the benefit of all people that on earth do dwell. This people was appointed to be a light to the nations (Gen. 12:1–3; 18:18; 22:18; Exod. 19:6; Isa. 19:24; 42:1, 4, 6; 49:6, 8; 66:18–21; cf. Zech. 8:13; Jonah).

According to an old and moving (thought hardly literal) church interpretation of Ephesians 2:14–18, the death of Christ has united the Jews and the nations into one people of God, because on the cross Christ spread his arms over both in an act of intercession for which he paid with his life. At Christ's table, not only is the reconciliation of individuals with God celebrated but also the reconciliation of all peoples with God and one another. For God willed and created universal peace by the mission and death of the Jew Jesus Christ.

During the Passover meal, Jesus spoke (according to the first three Gospels) of the *kingdom of God*: "From now on, I shall not drink of the fruit of the vine until that day when I drink it anew with you in the kingdom of God" (Matt. 26:29 and parallels). In Luke's report (22:16, 18, 28–30) this so-called eschatological outlook occurs, not once, but repeatedly. What happens now at Jesus' table in the circle of his disciples is to be understood as a firm promise, even a testamentary bequest, that Christ's people will be eating and drinking with their Lord at the eternal table.

The eschatological outlook does not add a strange topic to the "Passover of the Jews." Rather the words about Jesus' future combine the manifold Jewish hopes for the coming of Elijah, the gathering of the people from the dispersion, the rebuilding of Jerusalem and the temple, and the resurrection. Once more, Christ's coming, the Parousia, and Christ's eternal communion with God's people are the fulfillment of all promises and hopes given to Israel.

The meal instituted by Christ is not yet equal to, or to be identified with, the kingdom of heaven. Although the victory over all sin and the inclusion of the Gentile nations in God's covenant are proclaimed and celebrated at the table, the festive action retains an essential feature of the original, less glorious Passover celebration. Those assembled for the feast are people on their way, migrants who have not yet reached their promised destination. A pilgrims' meal is eaten, a rest is enjoyed, but the fulfillment of all promises and hopes is yet to come. The Supper expresses that yearning for the coming glory; open doors and windows and arms outstretched toward eternity are essential features of this meal, which barely anticipates the joys expected.

Several other features illustrate, on one hand, the cohesion of the Passover and Lord's Supper and, on the other, differences between the two. The presence of children, some of whom behave strangely, is reflected in the presence at Christ's table of the betrayer Judas (only in Luke 22) and of Peter, who will soon enough deny any association with Jesus. Absent is any hint of clerical mediation and manipulation. When Jesus Christ is proclaimed in the eucharist, the only priest is Christ himself, who has offered himself once for all time. Nobody, however properly ordained, can add anything vital to the meal as Christ celebrated and instituted it. However, two restrictions imposed upon the Jewish Passover festival are no longer valid. According to the New Testament, the Lord's Supper is to be celebrated not only once a year and not only in Jerusalem but all over the world and as often as the congregations assemble.

Conclusions

Jesus Christ was and is a Jew. He fulfills and does not abrogate the worldwide prophetic and priestly mission of God's chosen people. Pope John XXIII proved to be a wise and loving man when, early during the Second Vatican Council (1962–1965), he greeted visiting Jews with the words, "I am Joseph, your brother." The "one holy, catholic Church" of which the Apostles' Creed speaks is the daughter and sister of Israel. The concept of the one people of the one God exists in several forms; it is represented in today's world in the synagogue, the church, and the state of Israel.

The Lord's Supper cannot and must not be celebrated against the Jews, for spiritual communion between Israel and the church is essential to it. According to the Apostle Paul, "through Christ and in one single Spirit, the two have free access to the Father" (Eph. 2:18, author's translation). By "the two" Paul means (according to Eph. 2:11–13) the circumcised Jews and the uncircumcised Gentiles. Worship by Christians is the participation of Gentiles in the worship of the

Jews—this sharing is the work, the gift, and the effect of Jesus Christ and the Holy Spirit.

Whenever ecumenical unity between divided churches is seriously sought, when unity is supposed to be something better than a mere fusion of formerly competing business enterprises, Jews are indispensable participants in discussions about a common expression of faith. When Jews truly hope for the Messiah to come, who is promised to God's people, they trust in the Anointed One, who, according to the Christians' confession, has been born in Bethlehem and will come again on the last day. Christians, most of whom are of Gentile extraction, are in dire need of the presence, cooperation, and warning of the Jews. Otherwise, who will protect us Gentile Christians from forming a pagan symposium and therefore a fictitious church unity? Not even an agreement on the basis of the philosophical and sacramental thought-patterns found in the theology of Augustine and Chrysostom will solve the problem. For instance, the simple accumulation and preservation of most of the existing high sacramental and ecclesiastical doctrines (as represented by the World Council of Churches' Lima text, *Baptism, Eucharist, and Ministry*) is a device by which the churches try to boast of their riches rather than realize their poverty and repent of their errors and divisions. (For details, see the Epilogue.)

The following are among the liturgical consequences of the close relationship between the Passover and the Lord's Supper: (a) the abandonment of all altarlike structures in favor of real tables; (b) the participation of children, because such participation is not only permissible but necessary; (c) the combination of the liturgical act with a real meal, called agape in the early church; (d) a joyful and jubilant way of celebrating, including spontaneous oral, musical, or artistic contributions from as many inspired church members as possible; (e) the elimination of all elements of clerical dominion over the meal; and (f) the opening of the church and chapel doors for spontaneous and for regular intercommunion.

2

Communion with Christ Crucified and Risen

Public Joy Based on Christ's Death

Paul and the Corinthians

The terms *Lord's Supper* (1 Cor. 11:20), *Lord's table* (1 Cor. 10:21), and *communion* (alternative translation of 1 Cor. 10:16) were probably introduced into eucharistic literature by the Apostle Paul. Although other New Testament passages, especially the documents ascribed to John, mention ways and expressions of communion with Christ that are not restricted to sitting at the Lord's table (see, e.g., 1 John 1:3), Paul uses the term *communion* emphatically, though not exclusively, in his discussion of the Lord's Supper. In two chapters—1 Corinthians 10 and 11—the Apostle describes the Supper that Jesus Christ has instituted. Having concentrated on the institution texts of the Synoptic Gospels, we turn now to the witness given in the Pauline chapters about the meal.

How does Paul speak of the Supper? Three forms of diction can be discerned. Twice Paul quotes eucharistic formulas that the Corinthians may have known well (from Paul's or another person's teaching) before the first letter to the Corinthians arrived in their city. 1 Corinthians 10:16 (also perhaps the beginning of 10:17) and certainly 11:23b–25 (or 26) show that the Apostle presupposed the Corinthians' acquaintance with confessional or liturgical formulas. If they can be reconstructed at all, their wording may well have been: "The cup of praise over which we say grace . . . , the bread that we break . . . *is* communion with . . . ," and "the Lord Jesus on the night . . . in remembrance of me" or "until he comes." The two parallel rhetorical questions posed in 10:16 remind one of an analogous rhetorical question about baptism in Romans 6:3 ("Or don't you know that all of us who were baptized in [the name of] Christ Jesus were baptized in his death?"). Such a question makes sense only when the readers of Paul's letter(s) could answer affirmatively, on the basis of information received earlier. In 1 Corinthians 11:23 Paul explicitly states that he is using a formulated account handed down to the congregation in the name of the Lord.

To both quotations of eucharistic formulas, Paul adds an interpretive verse to clarify the sense of the preceding sentences: 10:17 as a whole or in part and 11:26, unless this verse belongs, together with verses 23–25, to the words of Jesus.

The third form of diction appears when scandalous misuses of the Lord's Supper make Paul turn to the Corinthians with urgent exhortations concerning the celebration of this meal. He wants the Corinthians to learn from Israel's worship (10:18) and to mend their evil ways (10:19–27; 11:17–22, 27–34).

Thus, what Paul writes about the Lord's Supper combines elements of confession, of narrative, of commentary, and of ethical (or practical) theology. Doctrinal inductions and deductions, definitions and systematizations, are not found in the eucharistic passages of 1 Corinthians 10—11. Perhaps if Paul had written to other congregations, he might—depending upon their needs—have placed other things in the foreground. The text of 1 Corinthians 10—11 does not contain a timeless doctrine on the eucharist; rather, specific practical problems are taken up and met head-on. Here, as elsewhere, Paul's theology is practical theology, conceived and expressed in the context of a congregation's worship and conduct. How much can be reconstructed of the situation in Corinth in Paul's time?

Among the Corinthians were people who today would be called high-church sacramentalists. They were convinced that through revelation, through the gift of wisdom and knowledge as mediated to them through baptism and the eucharist, they had received the Holy Spirit abundantly. They considered the Spirit, of which they were full, a guarantee of security and a protection from future condemnation. Probably—like Ignatius of Antioch (Epistle to the Ephesians XX.2) in the second century and the Catechismus Romanus (II.4.53) during the Counter-Reformation—they equated the eucharistic elements with a medicine of immortality (*pharmakon athanasias*). One evidence of the Corinthians' repletion with the Holy Spirit (cf. 1 Cor. 12:1–3, 13) was their worship service: almost everybody spoke in tongues and thereby proved to be a charismatic (pneumatic) person (1 Cor. 14). Another proof they found in their daily life: they felt so enriched, secure, free, full of new life, that they coined the phrase "everything is permitted" (1 Cor. 6:12; 10:23)—a phrase we might render as "anything goes." They behaved accordingly: some of them felt free to go, before or after celebrating the Lord's Supper, to banquets held in pagan sanctuaries (1 Cor. 10:19–22). Paul may have had in mind orgiastic or mystery cults in which bloody meat or blood in other forms may have been consumed and washed down with wine. When Paul speaks about "being partner with demons" (1 Cor. 10:20), he reveals his awareness of the demonic character of those cultic happenings.

Because of their sacramental and spiritual security, the Corinthians cared little or nothing about the social bonds and obligations that were respected among Jews and Christians, and even among Gentiles (1 Cor. 10:32). This lack of caring became shamefully public when they assembled for the Lord's Supper. First, a full meal was enjoyed by the richer and supposedly better people of the congregation. While the poorer church members, slaves and maids, small tradespeople, shopkeepers, and artisans, were still working, the richer Christians ate and drank what they had brought with them. Only later, when the so-called have-nots (11:22) arrived, was the Lord's Supper proper celebrated, including the blessing of the cup and the breaking of the bread, as described in 1 Corinthians 10:16; 11:26. The effect was a splitting of the congregation (Paul speaks of *schismata* [plural] in 11:18 [cf. 1:10] and *schisma* [singular] in 12:25). Thus the sacred meal had become a means of preventing certain church members from enjoying full communion with others: the poor members were made to feel despised and ashamed (11:17–22).

Paul's response to both misuses is hard and uncompromising—a devastating condemnation of the insult to the host, Christ, and at the same time a constructive aid to a decent and orderly celebration (cf. 1 Cor. 14:40). In 1 Corinthians 10:1–12 Paul begins his discussion of the Lord's Supper with sharp words—actually with thunderbolts. The section might be paraphrased this way:

You believe that being drenched in the Holy Spirit and fed with spiritual food makes you immortal? Look at the people of Israel! See what a baptism they had in the Red Sea! How the Lord was present in a cloud! How they were nourished with manna, the bread from heaven given to them by God! They drank from the rock—the rock that was Christ—that was with them, there and then, in the wilderness time! Indeed they believed in heavenly food and in the real presence of the Lord! But look how they displeased the Lord! They desired, chose, and did evil, and they were slain, their corpses left to rot in the wilderness [cf. Heb. 3:17; John 6:49, 58]. So much for sacramental security and conveyed immortality! Israel's history demonstrates that even a gift from heaven and trust in the Lord's presence can be useless when it leads to idolatry and scandalous conduct. Sacrament is not an alternative to ethics, but ethics is essential to it. Unless you stand firm amid temptations and God protects you anew every day, your security is self-deceptive, a sheer fiction, though it may be founded upon your faith in salvation by the sacraments.

To the Exodus prototype (10:6, 11) from the Old Testament, Paul adds a reference to an experience of the Corinthian church of his own time. In 1 Corinthians 11:29–30 he points out that "many" of the Christians in Corinth were sick or weak and that many had died. Concerning participation in pagan cultic meals, the Apostle reminds the Corinthians that God should not be provoked to jealousy: God does not tolerate the church's divided allegiance (1 Cor. 10:21–22; 2 Cor. 11:2; Eph. 5:25–27; cf. Rev. 19:7–8). The first commandment is still valid (cf. Luke 16:13: "You cannot serve God and mammon"). In our terminology, "You cannot dance at two weddings." What, then, is meant by exclusive communion with Christ?

1 Corinthians 10:16-17: An Important but Partly Obscure Text

A literal translation of 1 Corinthians 10:16–18 might be worded this way:

16a: The cup of praise over which we say grace—is it not communion with the blood of Christ?

16b: The bread that we break—is it not communion with the body of Christ?

17a: One is the bread!

17b: (Therefore) we who are many are one body,

17c: for all of us partake in one bread.

18: Look at the earthly Israel: are not those eating sacrificial meat in communion with the altar?

Paul expects these three rhetorical questions to be answered affirmatively.

Some observations based on historical-critical methods, especially of philological, literary, form-historical, and tradition-historical research, are necessary at the beginning of the interpretation of verse 16. Although they may seem all too technical, difficult, and cumbersome to be edifying, they represent scholarly highways and byways that may be useful for solving some serious problems of exposition.

The statements made in verse 16 over the cup, in which God is praised before the cup is passed around, and the interpretation of the bread, which is broken in order to be distributed, presuppose a solemn confession of the congregation: "*We* say grace over the cup . . . *we* break the bread . . . . This is communion with the blood and body of Christ." With their confession, those assembled at the Lord's table reflect the words spoken by Jesus during his last meal. Then and now the cup and the bread offer the occasion for explaining the sense and the purpose of the whole meal. Yet a difference should not be overlooked: according to the Western translations of the institution accounts in the Greek Gospels, the simple verb *is* was considered sufficient to link the cup (i.e., the wine offered in the cup) with the blood of the renewed covenant. The same verb is also used to connect the bread with Jesus' body. The congregation, however, responds by saying, "The cup is communion with . . ." and "The bread is communion with . . . ." Because Paul alludes (in vs. 16) to the church's confession in the context of the institution report containing Jesus' own words (11:23–25 or 26), it can be assumed that he considered the voice of the congregation a fitting and true rendition of the Lord's will. Still, is the phrase "is communion" less subject to divergent and divisive interpretations than the simple verb *is*? A study of the meanings of *koinonia* (communion) contributes to answering this question. First, though, the reversal of the sequence of bread and cup in verse 16 and the form and structure of the next verse require attention.

The cup and the words spoken over it precede the mention of the bread and the commentary on it not only in 1 Corinthians 10:16 but in two parallels to this unusual sequence: in the shorter Lukan institution text (Luke 22:16–19a) and Didache IX.2–3 ("*First* concerning the Cup. . . . *And* concerning the broken Bread [italics mine]"). Perhaps— though only in 1 Corinthians 10:16—Paul is using an early tradition of some churches in which the cup was given liturgical precedence over the breaking of bread. Such a custom certainly would contradict the assumption that the addition of the cup-word to the bread-word in the institution texts must be considered secondary, if not inauthentic. Less disputable, however, is another explanation: Paul may have placed the bread-body connection second because he intended to (and did in the next verse) continue his letter to the Corinthians with an additional comment on a very specific body.

Often, the whole of 1 Corinthians 10:17 is treated as an interpretation added by Paul to the traditional material to which he alludes in verse 16. The verse consists of three parts, which are worded as follows in the RSV:

a: Because there is one bread,

b: we who are many are one body,

c: for we all partake of the one bread.

As to syntax and style, it is rather strange that the RSV gives (in 17a and 17c) *two* reasons for the substance of the main clause (17b)— reasons that are either tautological or different, though complementary. Puzzling also is the fact that the meaning of *body* is not exactly the same in 16b and in 17b. Therefore, it is possible that verse 17 is, in part, composed of traditional, confessional phrases that may have been quoted exactly or paraphrased freely by the Apostle. Note also that the Greek conjunction *hoti* at the beginning of verse 17, translated in the RSV and elsewhere as *because*, on many occasions replaces a quotation mark in Greek literature. For this reason *hoti* in verse 17 need not be rendered *because*. Rather, "one [is the] bread" may well be a quotation (fragment?). Verse 17c then does not add a second reason for 17b that would compete with or duplicate verse 17a. Indeed, just as John 6:35–51 clearly affirms that Jesus Christ is the Bread (of Life, not simply ordinary bread or one loaf of bread), so also the phrase "one bread" may stem from a church confession or liturgy and have a strictly christological meaning. The combination of one bread and many as one body would then correspond to confessions such as one flock and one shepherd (John 10:16), and one body and one Lord (Eph. 4:4–5). Such statements are analogous to Old Testament utterances about the unique and inseparable bond between the one living God and the one elect people. Therefore, it is possible that 17a and 17b form an original unit, which was alluded to by Paul.

This verse would then (in analogy to the message of Ephesians and Colossians that the one head rules the body and keeps it together) give a *christological* answer to the question, "Why and how is the church one body, specifically the body of Christ?" Incidentally, a possible pre-Pauline origin of verse 17a and b would make it probable that the affirmations—the church is one body; the church is the body of Christ; the body of Christ is the church (1 Cor. 12:12, 27; Rom. 12:4–5; Col. 1:18; Eph. 1:22–23; 4:16; 5:30)—are not necessarily a Pauline, not to speak of a post- or *deutero*-Pauline, creation or innovation.

Turning to the varying meanings of *body*, observe that in 1 Corinthians 10:16 the term *blood of Christ* combined with the *body of Christ* most likely means—no less than in the texts of the institution of the Lord's Supper—Christ sacrificed, the crucified Lord. However, in verse 17b, the living organism of the congregation, without any reference to its suffering and death, is called *body*. Similarly, in 1 Corinthians 11:27 and 29, in close succession, the same two meanings of *body of Christ* reappear: in verse 27 guilt incurred by insulting the crucified Lord is mentioned, as the addition of *and blood* to *body* shows; verse 29 speaks of lacking discernment of the body (without reference to the blood!), that is, of the disregard and contempt for the unity of the congregation.

It is most likely that only the last of the three parts of verse 17 is a distinctly personal and original Pauline comment on the preceding words about the bread and the one body. This comment resembles or anticipates an element of the eucharistic liturgy contained in the Didache (IX.4): "As this broken bread was scattered upon the mountains, but was brought together and became one, so let thy church be gathered together from the ends of the earth into thy kingdom."

I turn now, finally, to one of the key terms of 1 Corinthians 10:16, the noun *koinonia* (communion). What exactly does this word mean? In verse 17 the verb *take part* (RSV *partake*; Greek *metecho*, which also occurs in 9:10, 12; 10:21, 30) may well explain the meaning of the noun. In addition, the plural *communicants* (*koinonoi*, partakers; in the RSV *partners*) illustrates the sense of communion (*koinonia*) in two dimensions: positively in the reference to the Old Testament priests (10:18), negatively in the reference to the intimate and horrifying bond between the banqueters and the idols in pagan sanctuaries (10:20).

Quite apart from Paul's different evaluations of the Jewish and the idolatrous kinds of having "communion" or "being in communion," he also hints at two divergent ways of attaining communion. The communion of the idol-worshipers with the demons was *created* by participation in temple banquets. When Paul writes, "definitely I will not that you *become* partners of the demons [emphasis added]" (11:20), he reveals that he is fully convinced of the causative, effective, creative—in short, sacramental—power of pagan cultic actions. Pagan sacrifices and holy meals miraculously join the offerers and the participants to the demons present in sanctuaries. However, the communion tradition in which Jewish priests stood was not created by their service at the altar and by eating the pieces of meat that they were entitled to take from the slaughtered animal, after the parts belonging to God (and in some cases before pieces to be given to those bringing the offering) had been set apart. Rather, says Paul, "they *are* in communion with the altar" (10:18). Being in communion with God's altar means communion with God by divine election, by birth into a chosen tribe, also by education and consecration, in short, because of the facts and events that preceded the service at the altar. The share in the sacrificial meat that they received from the altar was a sign of the community that they were privileged to enjoy, not a means of attaining it. In analogy, the Israel to whom Paul refers in 1 Corinthians 10:1–13 is God's people, not because they ate and drank bread and water miraculously provided by God in the wilderness, but by God's love, election, and revelation, manifested in the calling of the patriarchs and of Moses and by the liberation from Egypt.

Should now the Lord's Supper be *effective*, creative, causative, as pagan sacrificial meals indeed were, rather than *significative and proclamatory*, as Israel's preservation in the wilderness and the Jewish priests' participation in sanctified food?

Dictionary evidence concerning *koinonia* should help to answer this question. The Greek word means communion, fellowship, an act or a proof of brotherly unity, also participation or sharing. *Koinonia* signifies a communion between *persons*, one that may be founded on sex, friendship, educational, or economic bonds. For example, a common devotion to lofty ideas and high ideals may lie at the base of communion, as may the common possession of certain things, a common interest in plays, sports, or weapons. *Koinonia* is something spiritual and strictly *interpersonal*. However, it often includes a physical expression of unity. Hearing, seeing, and touching are mentioned in 1 John 1:3; handshaking in Galatians 2:9; and almsgiving in Galatians 2:10; Romans 15:26; 2 Corinthians 8:4; 9:13. Certainly today we would add kissing as an expression of love.

A positive conclusion can be drawn, together with a negative consequence. The Lord's Supper is intimate existential communion between the participants in the meal and the person of Christ crucified; I have already shown why the separate references to body (flesh) and blood poured out describe the death of Christ as a sacrifice on behalf of sinful humanity. Communion with Christ means, for instance: the death of the one Jesus Christ concerns so fundamentally those sitting at the table that they accept—to use Pauline terminology—that his death is their death; that his suffering makes them willing and capable of suffering with him; that his resurrection promises theirs; that their life is in him as he is in them—he *is* their life. In the Parousia they will be with Christ. Such elements and aspects of personal communion with Christ Paul unfolds in, for example, 2 Corinthians 4:10–11; 5:14; Romans 6:3–11; Galatians 2:19–20; Philippians 1:20; 3:10, 20–21; Ephesians 2:6; Colossians 2:9–13; 3:1–4; 1 Thessalonians 4:13–18. The unity with one single outstanding person is anticipated in the Old Testament accounts of the patriarchs, the stories and the psalms attributed to David that actually describe Israel's, or every pious Jew's, self-understanding; in the representative role of Goliath, whose death means the defeat of all Philistines; and in the equation of the "breath of our nostrils" with "the LORD's anointed" (Lam. 4:20). The communion with Christ that Paul describes when he speaks of himself is also proclaimed by the Apostle to Peter and other Jewish Christians who sit at one table with Antiochian pagan-born members of the congregation (Gal. 2:11–21) and in almost all his letters to Christians everywhere. Christ is one, and all those who believe in him are one with him and in him (Gal. 3:28; 1 Cor. 10:17a–b). Paul affirms in 1 Corinthians 10:16 that an act of worship that includes prayer ("praise"), saying grace and receiving, sharing, and consuming bread and wine belongs in this communion and gives it expression.

On the other hand, the word *koinonia* does not mean (unless Paul has imposed upon it a meaning strange to Greek-speaking people) a joining, a common essence or function of diverse *things*—be they physical or heavenly elements, forces, ideas, or symbols. The notion that the body and blood of Christ might enter a mysterious union with bread and wine, whether by changing their substances or by adding some heavenly matter, would require the use of a word other than *koinonia* (e.g., *metabole*, "transformation," or *mixis*, "mixture," or, in later technical sacramental and christological literature, *communicatio idiomatum*, "mutual enrichment of heavenly and earthly characteristics").

At this point I wish to answer an objection that is likely to be raised. In 1 Corinthians 10:3–4, Paul does speak of the "spiritual" (*pneumatikos*) food and drink consumed by Israel in the wilderness (RSV leads us onto a wrong track by translating *pneumatikos* as *supernatural*). Should Paul's reference to manna and water as spiritual substances mean that he considers bread and wine transubstantiated, transformed, or consubstantial with some heavenly matter, with the flesh and blood of Jesus Christ? Although the reference to eating the flesh and drinking the blood of Christ in John 6 will be discussed at some length in chapter 4, the meaning of *spiritual* in 1 Corinthians 10 can be clarified in a few words. *Spiritual* in verses 3 and 4 means "having a typological or allegorical sense." In verses 6 and 11, the Apostle says explicitly that the events in the wilderness were "typical" (in Greek, *typos, typikos*; i.e., prototypical and precedential). Not only the food and the drink are spiritual; so, too, is the rock from which the water flowed (vs. 4c). Spiritual, or pneumatic, interpretation points out, usually in the light of later revelatory acts of God, what was present but hidden in earlier events, words, and names. Some Roman Catholic scholars have called this sense of biblical passages the *sensus plenior*. That the rock was Christ is said explicitly in verse 4. Paul had no reason to postulate that in the wilderness the Israelites ate something other than material manna and drank something other than plain water, even when he was referring to the water that God had made to flow from the rock. Therefore, he does not implicitly affirm that in the Lord's Supper the Corinthians are eating and drinking, as it were, the Holy Spirit. He does not identify the Lord's Supper with a miraculous yet institutional way of conveying and receiving the Holy Spirit, that is, with baptism by the Spirit (as mentioned in, e.g., Mark 1:8; Acts 1:5; 1 Cor. 12:13), or with sealing by the Spirit (cf. 2 Cor. 1:22; 5:5; Eph. 1:14; 4:30).

Returning to 1 Corinthians 10:16, I wish to draw attention to as yet unsolved problems: *koinonia* may mean the *giving* or bestowing of a gift, as when Jesus *gives* the bread and wine to his disciples. It may also mean the *taking* and accepting of a gift. The words "take, eat . . . , drink . . ." in Matthew's and Mark's Gospels, and the command "do this in remembrance" in Luke's and Paul's institution reports emphasize human activity, as does Paul in 1 Corinthians 10:17c when he says "we partake." Further, it is not clear whether the giving or taking has a causative function in creating and establishing communion with Christ or whether it expresses (in the fashion of a signal, token, or proof) a relationship to Christ that has been founded and made valid on the cross (and in the resurrection) or through the Holy Spirit, the preached word, or faith. In the causative sense the Lord's Supper is an ever-new, saving miracle; in the revealing or confirming sense it is a signal and documentation of Christ's completed work.

Does verse 17 offer penetrating light that dissolves the obscurities of the use and sense of *koinonia* in verse 16? In fact, Paul's comment on verse 16 (given in vs. 17) is in some aspects equally ambiguous. Two different reasons and an adventurous combination of them seem to exist for demonstrating why the "one body" holds together many people.

(1) When verse 17a is read with 17b, only Jesus Christ, the One Bread in person, is the paragon, the giver and the gift, the sustenance and the perfection, of the many church members' oneness in and with him and of their unity with one another. Earlier, I called this argument *christological*. If Christology prevails in verse 17a and b, then the sharing of one loaf of bread (vs. 17c) is a public documentation and confession of the oneness and unity that is often proclaimed in Pauline writings, especially in Galatians 3:28 and Colossians 1:11 (and in 1 Cor. 12:3–14 by emphatic reference to the gift and work of the Spirit) *without* any mention of the Lord's Supper. The logic connecting 17b with 17c then corresponds to the logic of statements such as "They belong together and are good friends, for they share with one another what they possess." Obviously, the sharing expresses and confirms, rather than causes and effects, intimate community. In the interpretation of verse 16, as in the exposition of verse 17, the context must be kept in mind: maintenance of Israel in the wilderness and the firmly appointed Jewish priests' share in holy meat are signals rather than causes or means of salvation.

(2) On the other hand, if the "one bread" of 17a does not (in a manner parallel to John 6:35–51) designate Christ but the broken loaf of physical bread mentioned in (16a and) 17c, and if 17c rather than 17a describes the reason for being "one body" in and with Christ, Paul's reasoning is *sacramental*. In that case, he asserts that incorporation into the body of Christ is the essence and effect of the Lord's Supper and that it is graciously bestowed and gratefully accepted in and through the sacrament, just as communion with the demons (1 Cor. 10:20) is caused by pagan temple banquets. The traces of Canaanite worship that expert scholars have discovered in Israel's cult would then form a precedent for Paul's hellenistic transformation of an originally Jewish celebration and interpretation of the Lord's Supper.

(3) A combination of the christological and the sacramental arguments seems possible. Paul might have composed the three parts of
verse 17 because he intended to say that Christology issues in sacramentalism. If so, he wanted to teach that the mystery of Christ is extended, applied, and validated through the correlated mystery of the
Lord's Supper.

Two things are obvious. (1) The three (and maybe more) interpretations of verse 17 have borne ample fruit, that is, diverse liturgies and
doctrines of the Lord's Supper and scandalous divisions between
churches. (2) Using the structure and wording of this verse alone, one
can hardly make an indisputable choice in favor of one of the interpretations. Verse 17 resolves as little as the preceding verse the divisive
issues that have, since the early Middle Ages, torn the Christian community apart and made of the festival of communion with Christ an
occasion and means of mutual excommunication by official church
bodies.

However, another point of controversy is at least partially resolved
by verse 17. What or who is changed during the Lord's Supper? The
invocation (*epiclesis*) of the Holy Spirit is a fundamental element of
the Eastern Orthodox celebration and understanding of the eucharist.
This calling upon the Holy Spirit expresses the conviction that only the
Spirit of God can and will effect the miracle of changing (transub-
stantiating) bread and wine into flesh and blood. Similarly the liturgy
of the Roman Catholic mass contains a prayer for the coming and
creative activity of the Spirit. While in the Roman tradition the transubstantiation of the earthly elements is considered the effect of the
words of institution properly recited (*"hoc est corpus meum . . ."*), the
Spirit is called upon primarily to change the people who are assembled. Their unification and the renewal of their hearts and minds
stand in the center. Thus, the Spirit is expected to perform a personal
and social, rather than a material, miracle. In the Synoptic Gospels
and the Pauline eucharistic texts, the Holy Spirit is never explicitly
mentioned, although there are indeed many good reasons for the
churches, their liturgies, and theologians to emphasize the essential
and creative function of the Spirit in the Lord's Supper. It is probable
that the witness of 1 Corinthians 10:16–17, though it is silent regarding
the Spirit, implicitly supports the Roman Catholic rather than the

Eastern Orthodox liturgy and position. For these two verses do speak of the personal effect of Christ the Bread and the sense of the communal sharing of one loaf during the eucharist. Equally, in 1 Corinthians 12 the work of the Spirit in uniting *the church* (the one body of Christ having many members)—not a change affecting the physical elements—is extensively discussed.

In concluding the discussion of verses 16 and 17, I face a disappointing result, if not the failure of a mission. Taken by themselves, including the study of their vocabulary, syntax, logic, and alleged or real parallels in other religions, these loaded sentences fail to point a way out of the mists and quagmires in which eucharistic dialogues are still caught. However, other, possibly clearer statements in 1 Corinthians 10 and 11 may be helpful.

1 Corinthians 11:26: An Often Neglected but Clear Text

Every detail in 1 Corinthians 11:23–26 need not be discussed. The form and substance of verses 23–25 are so near the Synoptic institution texts that the interpretation offered in chapter 1 may suffice. However, there is one striking difference between Paul's account and the Synoptic records of Jesus' last meal: Paul speaks of "the night in which the Lord was handed over," but he does not mention that it was the night of the Passover meal. Should this omission demonstrate that my exposition of the words "this is . . ." "body and blood," "in remembrance"—dependent as it is on the Jewish Passover liturgy and the biblical meaning of remembrance—does not apply to 1 Corinthians 11:23–25? Might these verses prove that according to the earliest written tradition (Paul's!), and therefore perhaps in fact, Jesus' last meal was *not* a Passover meal? If so, Paul might indeed disqualify much of what has been said about the relationship of Passover and Lord's Supper, of Jewish and Christian worship, and of Israel and the church. However, this conclusion is precocious for at least three reasons: Paul does not explicitly deny the Passover connection; the Apostle does state, "As our Passover Lamb, Christ has been slaughtered" (1 Cor. 5:7); and Paul compares the Lord's Supper with a sacrificial meal, i.e., with the priests' sharing in the meat taken from the altar (1 Cor. 9:13; 10:18).

The three parts of 1 Corinthians 11:26 may bring into broad daylight all that has been left in the dark so far.

a: For as often as you eat this bread and drink the cup,

b: you proclaim the Lord's death,

c: until he comes.

Many German scholarly interpreters consider this sentence a "Pauline interpretament" (as some German scholars call it), i.e., an addition presenting the Apostle's own understanding of the preceding words of institution. More likely, verse 26 is the final part of the church tradition cited by Paul.

(1) The Greek verbal form rendered in RSV as "you proclaim" may as well be translated as the imperative "proclaim!" and may be considered a continuation of the words spoken by Jesus in verse 25. The imperative deserves preference because Paul would contradict facts if he named, of all people, the gluttonous and carousing Corinthian participants of the Lord's Supper the proclaimers of Christ's death. He may have called the Corinthians to order by an imperative and thus pronounced his own authority. Even more likely, he was evoking a specific tradition, which was not taken up by the Synoptics, saying that Jesus told the disciples not only to remember but also to proclaim him, that is, to celebrate him and his death by their meeting at his table. For the reader of Paul, as well as for the Apostle himself, an interpretation of the Lord's Supper according to Jesus' words would bear higher authority than an apostolic interpretation that at best would contain an opinion (1 Cor. 7:6, 10, 12, 40).

(2) 1 Corinthians 11:23–25 would be the one and only biblical version of a report on Jesus' Last Supper without an "eschatological outlook" if verse 26 did not belong to the institution text itself. It is unlikely that there ever existed in the early church an institution report without words pertaining to the future. Justin Martyr (in his *Apology* I.66.3) stands in flat contradiction to the biblical accounts and to the early Christian Didache IX—X by presupposing a liturgy of the Lord's Supper that does not refer to the coming kingdom. Still, perhaps in Rome such a curtailed liturgy was used.

(3) In 1 Corinthians 11:24–26 the transition from words in the first person ("This is *my* body. . . . This cup is the new covenant in *my* blood. Do this in *my* remembrance [emphasis added]") to words in the third person ("you proclaim the death *of the Lord*, until *he* comes [emphasis added]") may seem surprising. However, this transition does

not prove that Jesus is no longer the speaker. Several psalms (e.g., Ps. 23) freely change from praising God in the third person to addressing God directly in the second person. Institutional texts, especially 2 Samuel 7:11 and Psalm 132:13, change from *I* to *He* without indicating that a person, other than God, is the speaker. According to the Gospels, Jesus very often spoke of himself in the third person, especially when he called himself the Son, the Son of man, or the Lord. As Hans Lietzmann observes in his commentary on First Corinthians, in the Syriac liturgies after A.D. 200, 1 Corinthians 11:26 reads "*my* death" and ". . . until *I* come."

At any rate, verse 26 is a key to what Paul means in 10:16–17 by communion with Christ crucified. The conclusion of the institution text, of which Paul reminded the Corinthians, is so simple and clear, so free of obscurities and ambiguities, that its three parts are rich resources for describing the essence of the Lord's Supper and perhaps for finding alternatives to disputes over this meal.

You Proclaim the Lord's Death

The Supper is a *proclamation of Christ's death*. Many trite or pathetic ways to tell of the death of a person and to react to it are bypassed when the death of a person is *proclaimed*. A physician declares a person dead from natural or other reasons, and funeral arrangements are made. Lamentation over the loss or joy in the prospective inheritance may be evoked. Fear mixed with love can be the reaction to a tragic death. The death of a great poet, artist, inventor, or leader may increase the respect due to a great man or woman. The convictions, words, deeds, and sufferings, which adorned a lifetime, may be so confirmed and crowned that they begin to radiate to later generations. Protests and vows of revenge can be the reaction to the death of an innocent person. By imitation, followers can try to make a martyr's cause go on and reach faraway places and times. People may celebrate a tyrant's death by dancing on the grave. Finally, the death of a demigod calls for rituals in which dying and becoming, the divine fate and the human experience, are dramatically combined and boldly identified.

Though the Bible contains some examples of such dealings with death, none of them expresses exactly what Paul meant by the words "proclaim the Lord's death" (vs. 26b). For Paul the death of Christ was and is good news, and to speak of Christ crucified is, according to him, the only proper way to speak of the Lord, for all the wisdom of God and the sum of the gospel are enclosed in him (1 Cor. 1:18—2:16). "*Proclaim* the Lord's death"—during the Lord's Supper means that at this table are to be expressed the pleasure and the joy that are caused by the crucifixion. To proclaim means to announce publicly and clearly (rather than to whisper through cupped hands into the ears of an exclusive number of initiates) what has happened and the meaning of the event.

The eucharist is an occasion and a practical form for showing and confessing that Jesus Christ's death is totally different from a natural event, a criminal act, a tragic loss. It is not a reason to accuse, moan, or complain. Further, it is not an example that can be imitated by anyone.

What is the distinct essence of Christ's death and its impact upon those Christ has called together? Paul's answer is given in the passages of his epistles in which he calls Christ's death a sacrifice. As hinted at earlier, the writings of the New Testament mean something other than what is understood in general religious or secular parlance by the term *sacrifice*. The term signifies God's greatest gift to humanity: "He who did not spare his own Son but gave him up for us all, will he not also give us all things with him?" (Rom. 8:32). "Christ Jesus whom God put forward as an expiation by his blood" (Rom. 3:25; cf. John 3:16; 1 John 4:9). "As our Passover Lamb, Christ has been slaughtered" (1 Cor. 5:7). Those celebrating the Lord's Supper know the pain and shame, the horror and scandal, of Christ's death. However, they rejoice in the crucifixion and praise the slaughtered Lamb because God has raised from the dead the crucified Son and has accepted his intercession by enthroning him at God's right hand. In Paul's theology, as much as in the message of John, Hebrews, First Peter, and Revelation, the Crucified is always the raised and living Christ. The one who rules the church and the world and who will come again is the crucified Christ. Through Christ alone the godless are justified and reconciled, saved and given peace (Rom. 4:5, 25; 5:1; 6:5; 8:11; 2 Cor. 4:10–14;

5:14–15, 18–20; Eph. 1:19–23; 2:13–19; 4:9–10; Rev. 5). We have abundant reason to rejoice in Christ's death and to praise the slaughtered yet living Lamb.

The expression of joy and gratitude in 1 Corinthians 11:26 is described by the use of *proclaim*. This verb shows that even at the Lord's table the death of Christ concerns many more than a few chosen and believing people. According to Paul, all died when the one Christ died for all (2 Cor. 5:14). In Romans 5:6–10 Paul spells it out: Christ's crucifixion took place for those who are weak, the sinners and the enemies of God. In other words, Christ did not delay his death "for us" and for all until the moment at which we and all other people would be converted and gathered to his flock. Paul boasts of Christ's death because he knows that in and with Christ the whole world was crucified on Calvary (Gal. 6:13). This corresponds to the statement about Christ, the Lamb of God, who carries the sin of the world (John 1:29, 36). Proclaiming the death of Christ forbids an individual and egotistic, antisocial and particularistic celebration of the eucharist. This proclamation shows, commands, and promises that the Lord's Supper demonstrates the love of God for *all* creatures (not just those now present at the table). The Lord's Supper is, for this reason, a missionary event and action. The Lord's table is an occasion for and a center of evangelism rather than a selfish search for peace of the soul or joyful private satisfaction.

In all his epistles, and probably in his preaching as well, Paul was prone to use loaded theological terms (such as *sacrifice, justification, sanctification, reconciliation, redemption*) to describe the praiseworthy nature and effect of Christ's death. According to Galatians 2:11–21 it was during a crisis concerning the common meal of the congregation at Antioch that Paul first spoke of justification. However, when Paul quoted Jesus or said in his own words that the congregation does or shall proclaim Christ's death at the Lord's table, he hardly intended to say that the congregation must use Pauline vocabulary exclusively. Indeed, many other forms proclaim the death of Jesus Christ. The New Testament contains hymns in honor of the crucified and risen Christ (e.g., Phil. 2:6–11; Col. 1:12–20; Eph. 5:2, 25–27; 1 Tim. 3:16; 1 Peter 1:18–21; 2:21–25; Rev. 5:9–10, 12, 13)—hymns and confessions that in simple language sing the glory of Christ crucified.

The place for which such hymns were composed and at which they were originally used was most likely the Lord's table. Even in today's churches the singing of hymns is the most appropriate way to *proclaim* Christ's death.

Two other elements in the phrase "proclaim the Lord's death" require attention.

(1) It is neither the mystery of the mass or the church nor the special authority of priests that is celebrated. Those sitting at the table admire Jesus Christ alone and rejoice in his death—the one and final death for all the sins of all the world. How absurd it is either to convey to the meal part of the praise and glory due to (God and) Christ alone (e.g., by singing the praise of the mystery of the eucharist) or to treat the ordained clergy presiding at the table as specifically laudable and indispensable representatives of Christ and his sacrifice! It is enough to recognize that the Lord honors the congregation and all its members by inviting them to *his* table and to *his* praise. Their honor is to be honored by Christ. Paul discourages sacramental mysticism and all forms of mystery and personality cult. They draw attention away from the one true mystery: the love of God poured out in Jesus Christ and through the Holy Spirit upon Jews and Gentiles, upon those near and those afar.

(2) The proclamation is carried out when the bread is broken and the cup shared, according to Christ's command, by the assembled congregation and by each one of those who "eat this bread" and "drink from this cup." Before Christ's birth, prophets proclaimed his coming, and angels proclaimed his advent. After them Jesus Christ proclaimed the kingdom, even his own kingship. During his ministry he taught his disciples that he would rule by and from the cross. At the Last Supper, he was the herald of his own death, by speaking in separate sentences of his body and his poured-out blood. Then came Peter and John, and Stephen and Paul, who proclaimed Christ crucified in their own ways. Paul's proclamation took the form of oral preaching and teaching, of letters, of his apostolic suffering, and of some other "signs of an apostle." Disciples of this ambassador of Christ, along with other New Testament prophets, teachers, and missionaries, took up the message; they too became heralds, and some of them became martyrs. Finally, as emphatically stated in 1 Corinthians 11:26, the congregation at

Corinth is called upon to respond to the message preached, believed, and taken to heart. The letters to the Corinthians, like the other New Testament letters, have rightly been considered valid also for post-apostolic congregations, even of our time: *we* are urged to respond. To answer the challenge of the gospel means to take up the ball of proclamation and to carry it further.

Because of this verse, it should no longer be taught that the sacrament is primarily a form of God's or of the clergy's speaking *to* the congregation. At Christ's table it is the congregation that is authorized and enabled to speak. None of the New Testament institution texts mentions a duly ordained priest who has an indispensable function or monopoly between Christ and those sitting at the table. I repeat, verse 26 affirms that *all* the communicants—*together*—are heralds of Christ. This verse buries the distinction between clergy and laity and the dependence of the celebrating community upon the presence and function of a priest.

To make a long story short, verse 26 contains a clear-cut interpretation and application of the hitherto ambiguous key term of verse 16, that is, *koinonia* (communion). To belong to Christ, to be with him, to be assembled for worship in his name—this means at least three things at the Lord's table: (1) to give, in and as a community, thanks to God for the gift of Christ, (2) to comfort and strengthen brothers and sisters in demonstrating that Christ's death has created the bond of mutual love, and (3) to signal to all the world that God's work embraces all creatures and that the number of God's people is not yet complete. Communion with Christ at his table is therefore something that the participants themselves are *doing*, after and because they have been convinced and comforted by the Word of God and inspired by the Holy Spirit. Boldly formulated, the Lord's Supper is a human work that God has told us to *do*. It is not a work of law but a "work of faith" (cf. Rom. 3:28; 1 Thess. 1:3). Jesus' saying "Do this . . . take . . . eat . . . drink . . . proclaim" and Paul's explaining *koinonia* by "we . . . partake" (1 Cor. 10:17) give human activities surprising weight. Therefore the term *eucharist*, that is, *thanksgiving* (by the congregation), is an appropriate name for the Lord's Supper.

Where does this interpretation leave, or does it flatly negate, the "real presence" of Christ during this meal—the presence that plays so dominant a role in almost all liturgical and doctrinal expositions of the eucharist?

Until He Comes

1 Corinthians 11:26 ends with the words "until he comes." Indeed, *coming* can mean nothing but "real" coming. And the result of such coming is, without any doubt, "real presence." Still, the use of *real* is redundant. Does it perhaps reveal a depreciation of pure and simple presence? By discussing the ancient and the current theological understandings of Christ's so-called real presence, I hope to prepare the way for a proper understanding of statements about the heart and soul of the eucharist.

In liturgies used for the eucharist, in Bible commentaries, and in essays, monographs, and catechistic and dogmatic treatises concerning the eucharist, at least five ways of describing, locating, and glorifying the real presence of Christ can be distinguished. To some extent they are not mutually exclusive.

(1) According to a tradition from the time of Ignatius of Antioch and up to the World Council of Churches' Lima papers, the cleric administering the communion is the representative of Christ. Since Christ is not only the Bread of Life in person but also the giver of this bread (John 6:51) and since in the churches the ordained presiding officers act in Christ's name, the presence of Christ has been recognized and revered in the person standing behind or before the altar.

(2) Wherever the conviction prevails that bread and wine (through the invocation of the Holy Spirit and/or through the pronunciation of Jesus' exact words) change their nature, function, or significance, there the presence of Christ is believed to have its place and to find its "real" expression—upon the altar or the table or upon the lips of the communicants. Three or four variants can be distinguished: the real presence may be tied to the transubstantiation of bread and wine into the flesh and blood of Christ; or it is held that the natural elements are enriched through the hidden addition of flesh and blood; or it is taught that a transfunctionalization and/or transsignification of the products of God's blessing and of human labor takes place. In each variant, the gifts offered to God in the name of God, in miraculous combination with God's gift of Jesus Christ, are attributed much deeper reverence

than is shown toward the administrator(s) of the eucharist. Christ is present in the gifts on the altar, as indeed he is the peak and the sum of all of God's gifts.

(3) Rather rarely proposed and usually flatly rejected is the opinion that Jesus Christ spoke of (and pointed to) his disciples when he said the words "this is my body" and "this is the new covenant." As I mentioned earlier, a most interesting Greek variant reading of the Lukan account of the Last Supper has after the term *my body* no further comment on bread and cup. If the short reading is genuine (it is supported by a few very old Greek manuscripts and Latin and Syriac versions), Jesus indeed may have said as much as "I am present in (or as) the congregation." *My body* then means "you, my disciples, your communion with me." *Covenant* then signifies, as indeed it does occasionally in Qumran literature, "the covenant people." In that case, Jesus Christ would not be, as in his statement about the two or three gathered in his name (Matt. 18:20) or in his appearance on the Emmaus road (Luke 24:13–31), the third or fourth person in the company of two or three others. Rather, the gathered community would be the form of the Lord's presence on earth in the time between the ascension and the end of the world (cf. Matt. 18:20; 28:20). Indeed, some Roman Catholic and Protestant scholars affirm that in a certain sense Christ is the church, and the church is Christ. Especially 1 Corinthians 12:12 and Acts 9:4 are cited to support this equation. "Christ existing as congregation," the church as "the earthly-historical mode of the exalted Christ's existence"—in such ways has the presence of Christ been described, e.g., by Dietrich Bonhoeffer and Karl Barth. Pope Pius XII, in the Encyclical *Mystici Corporis*, and Anders Nygren, in his book on the church, use even more extreme formulations.

(4) Since the New Testament speaks of "Christ in me" or "in our hearts," the term *real presence* may mean Christ's spiritual inhabitation in human hearts (see, e.g., Eph. 3:17; Gal. 2:20). This presence occurs only, yet none the less powerfully and effectively, by faith. In faith the Lord's presence is experienced, faith is strengthened by the power of Jesus Christ, and through faith we are liberated from guilt, loneliness, and Godforsakeness.

(5) The Calvinist school of interpreting the Lord's Supper likes to

speak of the benefits of Christ's death, in which Christ is present and which are conveyed to the believers in the eucharist (see, e.g., Heidelberg Catechism, Questions 75–79). Indeed, without forgiveness of sins, eternal life, the Holy Spirit, unification with Christ, reconciliation, sharing, and peace, there is no Lord's Supper. Unless Christ is the cause, the giver, the substance of these gifts, they are devoid of reality, power, and validity. All the gifts of God are, according to Romans 8:32, included in the Son, whom God gave to us. If we remember this, Christ's presence at the eucharist is to be sought neither in the clergy nor in a specifically changed matter nor in any other tangible or intangible person or element. Instead, the heart of the matter is then the spiritual eating of spiritual food, which is done in faith. Obviously, Eastern Orthodox, Roman Catholic, and Lutheran theologians are speaking of the same benefits bestowed by and in Jesus Christ, as does the Reformed tradition. However, unlike Reformed teachers, Eastern Orthodox, Roman Catholic, and Lutheran liturgists and learned Bible interpreters make the benefits dependent upon an additional presence of Christ, which does not coincide with and is not to be identified solely with the benefits.

Better and worse biblical, historical, liturgical, and practical theological arguments do exist in favor of, or against, any one of the five alternatives. Yet the intensive discussion they deserve might lead us too far afield. An alternative, that is, a sixth way to recognize and praise the *Christus praesens* in the eucharist is, in chapter 3, shown to exist. Before I turn to Paul's statement on Christ's coming in 1 Corinthians 11:26, a survey of the essential elements in other New Testament utterances on the presence of Christ may be useful.

The Gospels never speak of *real presence*. When the Evangelists speak of Christ being present, they do it in the following ways. (1) They mention places, times, witnesses, and the effects of Jesus' coming in the stable of Bethlehem and being carried to Egypt; they report that he comes to the villages and towns in Galilee, Samaria, and Judea; he walks through the fields and is pressed by crowds; finally he carries the cross up to Calvary and is nailed to it. Phrases such as "he came," "he entered," "he was at," are used to describe his presence, and diverse forms of the people's reaction to it are recorded. When Jesus is present he can be touched lovingly or superstitiously or with violence. (2) Jesus will appear a second time. What we call the Parousia is expected by the writers and readers of the New Testament as an event as visible and concrete as his first advent or epiphany on earth. The clouds, the angels, and the trumpet sound with which he comes do not make his coming anything less than real. (3) The Christ who has appeared and will appear again, who has come and will come again, is a person surrounded by other persons. In appearance, Christ is as human as we are; he is distinct from the angels because he is the Son of man. In turn, the depth of his suffering and the majesty of his power and dignity as Son of God distinguish him among human beings. (4) He bears the features of a Jew, of the Suffering Servant, and he is called the slaughtered lamb. Because he has shouldered the sin of Israel, of the nations, and of his disciples, "his appearance was so marred" that he has "no beauty" or "comeliness" (Isa. 52:14; 53:2). (5) According to John 20—21 and to Acts 1:4 and 10:41, the risen Jesus took meals before or with his disciples, the so-called Easter meals. Paul does not mention these meals, though he may have heard of them. Certainly all accounts report that the risen Jesus was physically present during those Easter meals, e.g., on the Emmaus road or on the shore of the Sea of Galilee, as physically present as when he ate with sinners and fed the multitudes before his death. Rare are the indications that Jesus' presence after Easter was essentially different from that at the pre-Easter meals. However, his table communion with a limited number of disciples did not yet fulfill the riches promised for the new world. The disciples were promised that only after the Parousia would they eat together with the exalted Christ (Luke 22:28–30).

The New Testament stories, sayings, and parables concerning meals do not hint at a specific presence that would be different from Jesus' pre- and post-Easter presence in Galilee and Jerusalem, or from Jesus' advent in the Parousia. In sum the widespread references to Christ's real presence in communion, an issue that has caused so many and terrible disputes, have little or no foundation in the New Testament itself. Otherwise, as the Lima papers indeed affirm, the presence of Christ during the Lord's Supper would be a unique form of presence. If this were true, why are the common terms *presence* and *real* used to describe it? And why are the terms combined? In a discussion about real presence I heard the argument that real presence actually means symbolic presence because the symbol has and conveys more and deeper reality than what meets the eye and is touched by the hands. However, it would be difficult to demonstrate that biblical thought and diction are built upon this or another conception of symbol.

In 1 Corinthians 11:26 the reader looks in vain for the slightest trace of a statement that the Lord comes in, or by, the breaking of the bread during the Lord's Supper. A look at other Pauline utterances on Christ's coming affirms this. In verse 26 Paul, as elsewhere, speaks of the second coming of the Lord, the so-called Parousia (cf. 1 Thess. 4:13–18; Phil. 4:5; Rom. 13:11–12; 1 Cor. 7:29). The Apostle proclaims the close connection between the Lord's Supper and Christ's final (or second) coming. However, Paul avers only the direct relationship between the meal and the Parousia. He gives no signals that Jesus Christ comes in the person of the priest or in the substance of bread and wine. Indeed the Apostle does not discuss an invisible presence in the hearts of the believers that would be essentially or qualitatively different from Christ's presence during preaching, prayer, singing, and charitable acts; a secret identity between Christ and the assembled congregation is not proclaimed in 1 Corinthians 11:26. However, Paul does not deny a ubiquitous presence of the Lord. Jesus Christ is, for Paul, not an absentee landlord. The Apostle may or may not have heard of Jesus Christ's promise to be with the disciples always and everywhere when they assemble in Christ's name (Matt. 18:20; 28:20). If he knew of that promise, he certainly does not dispute it. For he speaks of the Son's revelation in the Apostles of Christ's being and speaking in and through his messengers, of his habitation in the hearts of all believers, through faith (Gal. 1:16; 2:20; 2 Cor. 13:3; Eph. 3:17). This spiritual presence is not restricted to the celebration of the eucharist; neither is it proclaimed as specifically concentrated during the Lord's Supper. According to 1 Corinthians 11:26, the common meal of the congregation is an open window and hands stretched out to the "second appearance" of Christ (Heb. 9:28), the Parousia. Actually, true love and communion always bear the marks of yearning for even more demonstration and realization.

Thus a limitation, even a transitoriness, of the church's celebration is to be acknowledged. The congregation that celebrates Christ and worships God retains all the traits of a migrating people. The church is filled with hope and trust that it will soon meet the coming bridegroom (2 Cor. 11:2; Eph. 4:13; cf. 1 Thess. 4:13–18; Matt. 25:1–13). Aware of imperfection, the congregation yearns to be cleansed by Christ and decked with Christ's garments of glory (Eph. 5:26–27; Rev. 19:8–9). Because it does not yet possess the future riches, the church cannot manipulate them, not even by quoting sacred formulas. Yet, while eagerly waiting for the Parousia, this community is very happy. The Lord's Supper is a pilgrims' meal, God's provision for people *en route*.

In the course of its history, however, the church has neglected or almost forgotten or abandoned to the care of some extremist groups the Parousia of Christ. This happened because of an inclination to be more concerned with the mystery of the sacraments administered by the church than with Christ, who is the mystery of God in person. The full power to be a witness to Christ, which is given to the church and to all its members, has been converted into the claim that the church is the rich and gracious mediator of grace and salvation. Thus the church has become blind to its essential poverty (cf. 2 Cor. 4:8; Rev. 3:17). The glorious baroque church buildings, with their gilded altar walls and lovely angels in the blue skylike ceiling, clearly bear one message: a person who has entered the church has already entered the heavenly kingdom. Thus the church, with its sacraments, seems to have fallen victim to the temptation to represent, if not almost to replace, the glory of God's own kingdom. In 1 Corinthians 11:26 Paul offers the alternative to this deviation: the yearning for the Parousia.

As Often as You Eat This Bread and Drink the Cup

Finally, the third part, actually the first line of 1 Corinthians 11:26, deserves comment: *as often as you eat this bread and drink the cup.* Is it the act of common eating and drinking at the Lord's table that is proclamatory and missionary? Or is the common meal instituted by Christ no more than an occasion for and a framework of proclamation, of an announcement that must be done orally, for example, by the loud reading of the institution text, by prayers and hymns, by sermons or homilies, by the recitation of a creed or the Lord's Prayer, or by testimonies of individual church members? It cannot be doubted that in the early church, just as today, several or all of these forms of oral proclamation had a legitimate place in the celebration of the eucharist. Yet Paul may intend more than the mere addition of reading, talk, declamation, and song to physical eating and drinking. In the New Testament the verb *proclaim* (also *evangelize* and *witness*) means more than to pronounce an entrusted message. An essential sense of the word is "to *be* a herald" or "to *behave* as a messenger." What is done orally, in speaking or singing, requires a specific total existence, including credibility gained, e.g., by suffering. John the Baptist was a witness not only because of the speeches he made. The place and food and garb chosen for his activity and finally his death as a martyr bore strong testimony. Paul's message is actual and existential in his life, his travels, his sufferings. Although the reasons for Jesus' meals with sinners is explained by words he spoke, his table communion with outcasts also spoke for itself. It was a sign language, a message conveyed by his behavior, saying clearly, "This man receives sinners and eats with them" (Luke 15:2). Because he associated with bad people so intimately as to dine with them, he was called "a glutton and a drunkard, a friend of tax collectors and sinners" (Matt. 11:19; Luke 7:34). A person's identity is clearly revealed by the company chosen for, or tolerated at, a common table. Therefore, eating and drinking together may speak more persuasively than words ever could.

In 1 Corinthians 11:24–26 the words "as often as you eat . . . and drink" are dominated by the preceding statements, "Do this in remembrance of me. . . . Do this, as often as you drink it [the cup] in remembrance of me." For this reason it is unlikely that the common eating and drinking are no more than an opportunity for oral testimony. Rather, the communal eating and drinking are actions by which the disciples remember and proclaim Christ's death, that is, by which they publicly demonstrate their communion with Christ crucified and risen.

How can eating and drinking effect such great things? This question—as Martin Luther asked in his Smaller Catechism—is all the more burning when we remember sayings such as the following: "The kingdom of God is not eating and drinking"; "flesh and blood cannot inherit the kingdom of God"; "the flesh is of no avail" (Rom. 14:7; 1

Cor. 15:50; John 6:63). However, Paul's and John's sentences against an eternal salvation of the flesh by the flesh do not preclude positive references to bodily acts, including the consumption of food. According to 1 Corinthians 10:31 and Colossians 3:17, eating and drinking and whatever Christians do are to be done "in honor of God," "in the name of the Lord Jesus as thanksgivings to God the Father through him."

The bread and *the cup* used in the eucharistic meal have specific functions. The eating of *the bread* distinguishes the Lord's Supper from other meals. Daily bread is received as a gift of God in the company of persons who have heard of God's gracious acts and want to give thanks for them. Gratitude for God's gifts is the basis for eating bread and drinking wine. Because the bread at the Lord's table is *broken* (1 Cor. 10:16; Acts 2:42, 46; 20:7), people eat at that table, not primarily for themselves, at best tolerating—as in a cafeteria—those who eat beside them. The Lord's Supper is a common meal, a community affair. The participants proclaim Christ's death and demonstrate their hope that Christ will return by sharing together what they have received from God, by accepting it gratefully, and by serving and loving one another. Confessions such as "I believe that Christ has died and was raised" are no good unless they are undergirded and verified by the sharing, serving, and loving that are exercised and demonstrated at the Lord's table.

For this reason the great concern of the so-called liberation theology for social and economic justice is more than simply supported by 1 Corinthians 11:26 (and the references in Acts, e.g., 2:46, to the breaking of bread). If the acts of sharing, eating, and drinking natural products are to be a proclamation of Christ's death, then the efforts directed toward properly rewarded production, adequate distribution, fair prices, and sufficent provision of daily bread must not and cannot be excluded from a genuine celebration of the Lord's Supper. Rather, social responsibility and action are the essence of the meal that Christ has instituted. Without active economic and political involvement, that is, without the breaking of bread in favor of the hungry, there is no communion with Christ (more on this theme in ch. 3).

The function of *the cup* from which Christ's guests drink complements the use made of the bread. In the Bible, as elsewhere, the drinking of wine demonstrates the need or the permission to be glad, to relax, and to forget the misery in which one is caught (see Ps. 104:15; Prov. 31:6–7). A cup of salvation is mentioned in Psalm 116:13: the people of God need not always eat and drink with tears in their eyes. Especially the book of Deuteronomy (e.g., 12:7; 16:11) insists upon the festival and joyful character of the sacrificial meals, which shall be held at the central sanctuary, in Jerusalem.

And yet, more than joy is meant by drinking the cup in 1 Corinthians 11:25–26. The cup that will not pass Jesus by, according to the Gethsemane story (Matt. 26:39, 42), and the cup that he *and* his disciples have to drink, according to Matthew 20:22–23, is the cup of God's anger (Isa. 51:17, 22; Jer. 25:15–18; Lam. 4:21; Ezek. 23:31–34; Hab. 2:16). To drink this cup means to suffer. Although the cup offered and drunk at the Lord's table is a cup of victory and joy, it presupposes and includes the cup of suffering. Those who drink it are aware of the price Jesus paid for the liberation of the Jews and the Gentiles. Only after and through his suffering did he become their Savior and enter glory (Luke 24:26, 46–47). By drinking the cup offered to them, the disciples were expected to show their readiness to suffer with Christ. According to the whole of the New Testament, especially to Paul and the book of Revelation, no one can be a trustworthy witness to Christ crucified who does not bear a share in the messianic sufferings (2 Cor. 1:5, 7; Phil. 3:10, 20–21; Col. 1:24). A Christian is a joyful herald of the crucified Lord, a brave witness to the necessity and the glorious effect of the terrible death of Christ.

To summarize, eating bread that is and remains bread and drinking wine that is and remains plain wine—these material, bodily, palpable actions are not too little, too trite, too contemptible, to serve a magnificent purpose. Whoever follows Christ's example and shares bread with a neighbor, whoever acknowledges that the only way to enter the promised glory is through much suffering, proclaims the death of the Lord and demonstrates living and true communion with Christ.

Not in vain do natural products and elements, even bread and wine, play a vital role in the eucharistic proclamation of Christ crucified. This use of bread and wine transcends the exclusively physiological, psychological, or sociological functions that these elements have for the benefit of humankind: this use manifests the cosmic relevance and impact of Christ's death. Seemingly marginal as well as indispensable things and events, even food and drinking and eating, are deigned to be included in divine worship. God, in the acts of creation and redemption, cares not only for human beings. Not only persons are glad when they are freed and hear of God's mighty acts and are made witnesses to them. According to the books of Psalms and the Prophets, the heavens and the sea, the fields and the trees, roar and sing with joy and clap their hands; mountains and hills explode in jubilation and jump like little lambs—all of them praise the Lord and all the Lord's works (Pss. 96:11–13; 114:3–7; Isa. 49:13: 55:12; cf. the apocryphal Prayer of Azariah and the Song of the Three Young Men, vss. 35–59). In the Lord's Supper cosmic elements are used and participate in saying thanks to God and enjoying communion with Christ.

3

Communion Among Christ's Guests

The Honor of Those Despised

Christology and Social Ethics

As mentioned earlier, more than one thing was wrong when the Corinthian congregation celebrated the Lord's Supper. Alongside the false security based upon a gross sacramentalism that seemed to permit people to participate in feasts to honor idols yet enjoy communion with Christ at Christ's table stood flagrant social misconduct. A split was created and tolerated in the church between the rich and the poor, between the common meal, meant for fellowship and the filling of one's stomach, on one hand, and the celebration of the Lord's Supper proper, on the other. While the richer Christians were overfed and drunk, the have-nots went hungry and were put to shame (1 Cor. 11:21–22). In 1 Corinthians 10 the threat to communion with Christ is the main topic; in chapter 11, attention is focused upon the dangerous cleavage among the members of the church.

However, in 1 Corinthians 10:17, the social dimension of the Lord's Supper is mentioned; in 1 Corinthians 11:23–26 communion with Christ crucified and exalted is the central theme. Therefore the two topics of chapters 10 and 11 are interdependent, not strictly separated from each other. According to 10:21 the Corinthians are "not strong enough to" ("you cannot" in the rsv) participate both in communion and in idol-feasts, and according to 11:20 it is "impossible" (Greek *ouk estin*) for the Corinthians to celebrate the Lord's Supper as long as their treatment of the poor is a public shame. This means nothing less than that there is no, not even a sacramental, communion with Christ when the social community is considered irrelevant or of secondary import and is in fact broken up. The relationship of the two communions is like that between the love for God and the love for one's neighbor. In 1 John 4:7–12, 19–21, it is shown that the two love relationships, though they must be distinguished, cannot be separated or exist apart from each other.

When Paul describes the disorder that besmirches the celebration of communion at Corinth, he seems to be boiling with anger. Certainly he attempts to moderate his diction when he twice affirms "I do not commend you in this" (11:17, 22); when he ascribes his awareness of the Corinthian situation to hearsay, which he believes (only?) partly (11:18); and when he suggests that the current evil state of affairs will help to reveal who is a genuine Christian (11:19). Yet he states that the Corinthians meet at table "not for the better but for the worse," and he flatly denies that it is the Lord's Supper that is celebrated in their midst (11:17, 20). He calls the banqueters' behavior "unworthy," "guilty of profaning the body and blood of the Lord" (vs. 27), and he goes so far as to say that God's own (not only Paul's) judgment condemns those misusing the Lord's Supper (11:29, 32, 34).

In the same context, in verse 30, Paul mentions that many among the Corinthians are "weak and ill, and some have died." Is he so self-righteous and malicious as to proclaim, in the face of bed-bound and crippled persons or of open tombs, "Here you see how God punishes immoral and antisocial conduct"? This verse can be explained in other ways. The Apostle may be saying that the bread and wine consumed at the Lord's table are not a medicine of immortality, securing health and life. If this is the case, he is implicitly admonishing the Corinthians to seek the common good rather than a private benefit at Christ's table (cf. 10:33). Or Paul may be encouraging those among them who humbly accept acts of divine judgment, because (here Paul may be alluding to a rabbinic teaching) those chastised in the present will not be eternally condemned in the future. "If we judged ourselves truly, we should not be judged. But when we are judged by the Lord, we are chastened so that we may not be condemned along with the world" (11:31–32).

In summary, Paul's edifying statements in chapter 10 about communion with Christ are followed in chapter 11 by words that warn and admonish the church. Here Christology issues in ecclesiology. The doctrine of the church, in turn, is practically identified with social ethics; it shapes Sunday worship and daily life equally. As I observed in chapter 2, the term *body* is used in different senses; in 10:16 and 11:24–25, 27, *body* is complemented by *blood*. The combination of the terms, Christ's *broken*, or *given*, *body* and Christ's *poured-out*, or *covenant*, *blood* designate Christ's sacrificial death. In 10:17 and 11:29, however, where the blood is not mentioned, *body* is a sociological concept and means the living organism of the church. The christological utterances are crowned by the proclamation that he will come (11:26); the ecclesiological, social, and ethical exhortations are introduced by the formula "when *you come* together" (RSV uses varying translations: "when you come together"; "when you assemble"; "when you meet together"). The first use of the verb *come* occurs only once (in 11:26), the second five times (in 11:17, 18, 20, 33, and 34; cf. also 14:23, 26). As communion with Christ, according to 10:19–22, excluded and prohibited association with idols and their worship, so now is dissociation from fellow Christians forbidden.

Does this mean that a *gospel* of the Lord's Supper (as mainly proclaimed in ch. 10 but also in 11:23–26) is followed by a *law* of the same meal? Or is the Lord's Supper similar to Janus, looking at the same time in opposite directions, or to a sheet of paper having two sides? Does the Lord's Supper have two poles on one axis around which it spins? Or should it be compared to an ellipse, which has two foci? Certainly all mechanical comparisons are even more absurd than the division between gospel and law, or the separation of the love for God from the love for neighbor.

No doubt, according to most verses in chapter 11 the Lord's Supper must be understood as an ethical act and event. Ethics is much more than an implication or a consequence of the Lord's Supper.

Rather, ethics is its home, its framework and purpose, perhaps even its essence. The celebration is, according to Christ's words, a deed of the disciples: "Do this in remembrance of me . . . when you eat and when you drink this. . . ." But does not ethics sometimes have a legalistic bent, a slant toward psychology and sociology rather than toward the Lord? In chapter 11 the ethics of the Lord's Supper unfolds in an evangelical way; we are shown that it is good and useful for the community and for each one of its members. Ethics is at the core of the gospel when its teaching is determined by the fact that Christ is Lord, that the church is Christ's people, and that each Christian has a specific function in the common praise of God and the public witness to believers and unbelievers.

Unequal Church Members

While Paul denounces the scandalous Corinthian misuse of the Lord's Supper, he lays the foundation of a better celebration. He begins to do this as early as chapter 8, and he carries it through the end of chapter 14. Each of the chapters in 1 Corinthians 8—14 discusses a common theme—though with variations.

In chapter 8 Paul treats the question whether the eating of meat is permitted when the sale of the meat is preceded by a ritual slaughtering of the animals in pagan temples. Those strong in faith and rich in knowledge are sure that such meat can be eaten; they are convinced—and rightly so—that an idol is nothing. Paul, however, urges those strong in faith to renounce their liberty lest by the misuse of their freedom they destroy the consciences of the weak, whose innermost conviction prevents the buying and eating of such meat. Paul argues that Christ has died for the weak; the Lord is their special protector. To sin against them is to sin against Christ (8:11-12).

In chapter 9 Paul points to himself as an example (cf. 1 Cor. 11:1) of a total yet humble servant of the Lord. Certainly God has bestowed rights and privileges upon the Apostle—but Paul prefers death to insistence upon his privileges. He was taken into Christ's service to be a *servant* of Jews and Gentiles: "To the weak I became weak, that I might win the weak" (9:22). Running his course like a good long-distance runner, he fights mainly himself, not others.

According to 1 Corinthians 10:23—11:1 the responsibility for the edification and the strengthening of the weak excludes the misuse of the freedom granted by God. God is praised only by conduct, including eating and drinking, that contributes to the advantage of many, of the community rather than the self (10:31–33).

In 1 Corinthians 11:2–16 Paul discusses the temptation of married women to use the congregation's worship as an opportunity to demonstrate emancipation. Their dress in the assemblies has made them look like certain unmarried ladies from harbor pubs and other love-temples in the city of Corinth. In analogy it would cause more than raised eyebrows if married female church members of all age groups attended European and North American worship services, clad in bikinis and having removed their wedding rings. Paul expects the women in the congregation to express voluntary subordination and respect for decency. He advises specifically that the married ladies of Corinth wear something in their hair or on their heads to show that they are married, as customary in Jewish worship. Paul considers behavior in the meetings of the congregation the example for everyday conduct. Note that praying and prophesying—the gifts bestowed by God upon women as well as upon men—are not questioned, reduced, or prohibited by Paul's call to humility and decency (cf. 14:34–36, 40).

A new, special topic is introduced in chapter 12. In chapters 8—11 "food offered to idols" (8:1) is the theme; spiritual gifts (and/or inspired persons) are the focus through chapter 14. According to chapter 12 the congregation is a unity in diversity and a diversity in unity. The ground of the essential and innermost combination of oneness with plurality lies in God: God is God the Father *and* the Lord Jesus Christ *and* the Holy Spirit. The same manifoldness is essential to the congregation (1 Cor. 12:2–11). Each of the church members has received a gift of the Holy Spirit, which is to be used, not for private benefit or pride, but for the common good. First the living organism of a human body, composed of many members and dependent upon each member's contribution to the whole, is chosen for comparison. Then, from verse 12 onward, Paul goes beyond comparison: not only does the congregation resemble a human body; it *is* the body, the body of one person, "the body of Christ." To present only the result of arguments too complex to be unfolded here, this means that the church is the missionary manifestation of Jesus Christ's life and rule. As in Old Testament anthropology the body is related to the soul, so the church is related to Christ the Lord (in 2 Cor. 11:2 and Eph. 5:25–27 the church is described as Christ's bride).

Among the parts of the body, some are weaker yet indispensable; those considered less honorable are invested with greater honor; those deemed unseemly are given more than ordinary seemliness. God has given "greater honor to the inferior" (1 Cor. 12:22–25). The diversity that God created between weak and strong, between superior and inferior, was intended neither to produce division nor to evoke the contempt of some persons for others. God's own intention is mirrored in the human need for mutual care and the pleasure derived from the interdependence of all members of the body. Verses 22–25 remind the reader strongly of the description of the have-nots who were put to shame at the Lord's table (1 Cor. 11:22).

Chapter 13, the best-known chapter in First Corinthians, speaks of love for one's neighbor—never in imperatives of direct exhortations, but always in a radiant, hymnic style. To show how splendidly this chapter fits into the context of chapters 8—14, I have chosen a somewhat unusual way of interpreting—by asking, to what sort of person do we owe love (cf. Rom. 13:8). That person—as we learn in 1 Corinthians 13:4–7—needs patience and kindness; that person invites zealous observation and radical correction; that person, quite simply, makes a miserable figure. That same person is irritating, almost compelling an observer to compose a catalogue of vices or evil deeds. At the beginning of Ephesians 4, Paul's words "Bear one another" describe that neighbor as a load. Similarly, at the beginning of Galatians 6:2, he says love is to "bear one another's burdens." The neighbor bears an all too heavy burden; perhaps the neighbor is also a burden to himself or herself. Reasons to have hope or faith for such a person seem far out of reach. That person is just a pain in the neck from which every self-respecting person hopes to be liberated at the earliest possible opportunity. Paul, however, praises the love for that man, that woman, that child (cf. Rom. 12:9–21; 13:8–10; Gal. 6:2; Eph. 4:2; 1 Thess. 5:14).

Obviously, love is not a virtue that can be applied equally to this or that subject. Rather, the content and substance of love consists in human beings, those who may be hard to bear because of their specific character, conduct, and public repute. This means that to love is to accept just such an unlovable person. Humanity as such, all people of the world, or faraway groups that suffer hunger and injustice cannot really be loved. A neighbor or a family member, even an enemy, who has to be loved according to God's will, is always a person known well and loaded with specific, perhaps repulsive, idiosyncrasies.

Finally, chapter 14 describes the richness and the problems of talking in tongues and prophesying during the assemblies for worship. The Apostle has no objection to the display of enthusiasm, yet he insists that *all* members of the congregation be exhorted, encouraged, and instructed by it. His special concern, actually the criterion of edifying worship, according to verses 22–25, focuses upon two kinds of visitors to the worship service: the unbelievers who have come into the assembly, and the apprentice Christians, the stumbling Christians, who have sometimes disturbed the worship and who are called *idiotai*. Most likely these two groups were assigned a special place in the rear of the congregation, just as the publican was in the synagogue (see Jesus' parable of the Pharisee and the Publican, Luke 18:13). Paul says that unless the nonbelievers and the *idiotai* can understand what is going on and unless they have a chance to be led to repentance before God and before the other worshipers, the whole worship has missed its purpose and is no good.

The common theme in chapters 8—14 can be spelled out as follows: among the manifold people who form the congregation and "come together" for worship some are supposedly inferior to the others. Those who feel superior tend to despise, belittle, override, or ridicule the others. Paul, however, protects the people who are treated as inferior.

In First Corinthians, the composition of the two groups discerned by Paul seems to vary from chapter to chapter; several polarizations within the congregation are described—the strong and the weak in faith, the rich and the poor in knowledge, those with a narrow and those with a wide conscience, and Christians who are Jewish-born and those who are of Gentile origin. Prominent church leaders stand opposite despised church members. Loud talkers are distinguished from shy listeners. In other chapters of his letters, Paul distinguishes male and female, parents and children, masters and slaves, but only in First Corinthians does he mention that disparate groups threaten to divide Christ and to split Christ's body, the church (1:10; 11:18; 12:25).

Elsewhere, Paul meets such distinctions and divisions head-on by saying that before God "there is no difference," that all people are sinners, justified only by grace, and that all are one in Christ (Rom. 3:23–30; Eph. 2:1–3; Gal. 3:28; Col. 3:11; 1 Cor. 12:13). Galatians 2:15–16 does not contradict but complements this proclamation of Paul—only, however, when the rendering of the Greek text that is found in the rsv and almost all Bible translations is replaced by the equally literal rendering of the original text: "We, being sinners of Jewish origin not of Gentile extraction . . ." are justified by Christ's faithfulness. However, in 1 Corinthians 8—14, at least three surprises lie in store. (1) Instead of emphasizing that all Christians are equal, the Apostle stresses the differences between them. He declares it necessary that inequality exist between various groups: "There must be factions among you that those who are genuine among you may be recognized" (11:19). Individual Christians and the groups they form are not equal, nor are they simply interchangeable, as are, for example, grains of sand (as long as they are not individually scrutinized). (2) Though Paul feels entitled to count himself among those rich in faith, the high and mighty, he chooses the side of those who are considered weaker and who are treated with contempt. He admonishes the congregation to respect and honor them, to prefer them to the strong and the rich. (3) Unlike his proclamation of equality in other letters, Paul's statement in chapters 8—14 seems to say that some members of the congregation are "more equal" and thus deserve more honor than others (see esp. 1 Cor. 12:23–24). This seemingly absurd statement calls for clarification.

The Most Honored Guest

On the grounds of Galatians 3:28 ("There is neither Jew nor Greek, there is neither slave nor free, there is neither male nor female; for you are all one in Christ Jesus"; cf. 1 Cor. 12:13; Col. 3:11) we presuppose that Jesus Christ is the source of and the criterion for the church's unity and the members' equality. Still, the question must be asked: to whom are they equal, or whom do they resemble most? In First Corinthians two answers are given: they resemble Jesus Christ, and they correspond to the composition of the congregation as a whole.

(1) According to Paul, Christ became weak, poor, despised, a scandal, and a foolishness to human reason, experience, and social standards, in order to come to those who are weak, poor, despised, who are considered scandalous or foolish, and who are treated as social outcasts. He came to them to be with them and to redeem them. "Though he was rich, yet for your sake he became poor so that by his poverty you might become rich"; "he was crucified in weakness, but lives by the power of God"; "the foolishness of God is wiser than men, and the weakness of God is stronger than men" (2 Cor. 8:9; 13:4; 1 Cor. 1:18–25). Therefore, those poor and despised in the congregation resemble the weak and crucified Lord, who is proclaimed through the Lord's Supper. They are more like him, closer to him than are those who boast of their knowledge, their faith, their strength, their leadership, their charismatic eloquence, their capabilities, and their riches. They may thus be called "more equal" than others. They are more equal *to Christ*.

(2) Paul states in 1 Corinthians 1:26–28 that, within the city of Corinth, among those called by God to the congregation, there are "not many . . . wise according to worldly standards, not many . . . powerful, not many of noble birth; but God chose what is foolish in the world to shame the wise . . . what is weak . . . to shame the strong . . . what is low and despised in the world, even things that are not, to bring to nothing things that are." As foolish, scandalous, and outcast as Christ is in relation to the world, so is Christ's congregation within the city. And what the congregation is within the city of Corinth is reflected as in a mirror by the state of the poor and despised at the Lord's table in relation to the rich, who enjoy their big banquet before the have-nots join them. Those poor and despised within the congregation are more equal to the essence and existence of the church as a whole than are those who hold positions of power, who consider themselves rich, and who act accordingly. For the poor are manifesting to the church and to the world that Christ has chosen and assembled the weak, the despised, and the condemned.

At the Lord's table both the resemblance to Christ and the expression of the church's essence and mission are decisive. The Lord's Supper is the festival of and for Christ crucified. This "festival of fools" declares publicly the constitution of the church. To remember and proclaim Christ's death and to stretch out human hands and hearts toward his coming, the diverse members of the church "come together." Because the weak and the poor and the little ones in the congregation stand under Christ's—not only Paul's—special protection, because they resemble him more than their strong and rich counterparts do, the Apostle Paul scolds those who despise and dishonor the poor. They sin against the body and blood of Christ (i.e., against Christ sacrificed on the cross) when they ill-treat their poor brothers and sisters (cf. 1 Cor. 8:11-12). They are "unworthy" to sit at Christ's table (11:27) when they despise the company of the have-nots. They show contempt for the whole congregation when they do not discern who they are and what the church is—the "body of Christ" (11:28-29; 12:12-13, 27), the company of miserable but forgiven sinners that has been assembled by Christ and is held together by Christ and the inspiration of the Holy Spirit (12:1-3). Those who feel superior to the weak and poor invite God's judgment (11:29-30). However, hope exists even for the rich: if they accept what they are in God's judgment, if they examine and properly adjudicate themselves, they, too, will be saved (cf. 5:5). To avoid falling under the future condemnation of the world, they had better accept the judgments experienced now as a preservation from eternal damnation (11:28-32, 34).

Toward the end of his discussion and admonition concerning the Lord's Supper, the Apostle writes, "when you come together to eat, wait for one another" (vs. 33a). No doubt the rich have to wait for the poor, but the rich are also given a chance: they, too, will be *waited for*. What the RSV translates *wait for one another* can also be interpreted *wait upon one another*, or even better and more literally, *receive* or *accept one another*. The expectation of the coming Lord is expressed in the practical conduct of the church members when the neighbor is received. As Christ has accepted sinners, so the members of the congregation are to receive each other mutually (cf. Luke 15:2; Rom. 14:1, 3; 15:7). According to Matthew, Jesus not only told his disciples to receive the little ones (e.g., the children) but added that in this way he would be received himself (Matt. 10:40-41; 18:5). "As you did it to one of the least of these my brethren, you did it to me. . . . as you did it not to one of the least of these, you did it not to me" (Matt. 25:40–45).

In summary, although I felt it necessary to speak out in chapter 2 against narrow sacramentalists and their notions of the presence of Christ and the effect of the Holy Spirit, neither the time nor the worship of the church between Christ's ascension and return is devoid of Christ's presence entirely. Christ is present in the person of the little and weak brother and sister at the Lord's table and in daily encounters. Maybe the little ones should be called messengers rather than representatives of Christ. When the messenger is received, Christ is received and present. "He who receives any one whom I send receives me; and he who receives me receives him who sent me" (John 13:20; cf. Matt. 10:40–42; 18:5, 10; 25:40–45; Gal. 4:14).

The existence, the coming, and the recognition of such neighbors are gifts of God. Neither Christians nor non-Christians can elect, produce, or shape them. People do not feel, nominate, or make themselves little brothers or sisters. The recognition and acceptance of persons who resemble Christ and reflect the essence of the church more than others is not decided by democratic election or by an aristocratic church board. Recognition and acceptance cannot be organized or forced upon anyone. The eyes must be opened and the heart inflamed, as were the eyes and the hearts of the disciples near Emmaus. Different people at Christ's table may recognize and treat one another as special envoys of Christ. A Samaritan may become the neighbor of a Jew by showing mercy to the Jew and thereby resembling Christ.

However, no one is entitled to consider the neighbor an object, an *it*. Those sent and given by the Lord are neither a sacrament nor a means of grace, neither a mirror nor a transparency. To treat them as such negates the uniqueness and dignity of each one of them.

It is equally absurd to prevent from sitting at the table any person who is invited by Christ and desires to follow Christ's call. Those very suspect or condemnable persons may be messengers of Christ. It does not matter, for instance, whether their sacramental convictions are considered (by the majority or by the leader of the congregation) too high or too low, whether their consciences are strong or weak, whether their moral qualities are a shining example or a sign of great weakness.

According to 1 Corinthians 5 the Apostle Paul himself, in the name of the Lord and the Holy Spirit and in convening with the congregation, exerted a temporary church discipline for the final salvation of a scandalmonger. The institutional discipline, described in Matthew 18:15–18, hardly implies that of all things the Lord's Supper is the proper occasion for excommunication.

"Wait for one another" (1 Cor. 11:33)! "Welcome one another . . . as Christ has welcomed you" (Rom. 15:7)! "Who is weak in faith, welcome him, but not for disputes over opinions" (Rom. 14:1)! Much more than condescending tolerance is meant by these statements. The context of each of these sentences speaks of love. *Love* for one's neighbor is not only an ethical corollary or implication of the Lord's Supper; it is the form and substance of the celebration of Christ crucified, who "loved us and gave himself for us" (Gal. 2:20; Eph. 5:2, 25). By the time of Ignatius (see his epistle to the Smyrnaeans VIII.2; epistle to the Romans VII.3; cf. epistle to the Trallians VIII.1) in the second century, the Lord's Supper was called *Agape*. Despite the misuse of Agape celebrations, of which some readings of 2 Peter 2:13 and certainly Jude 12 speak (cf. 1 Cor. 11:21), the meal to which Christ invites is in essence a festival of love—love for one's neighbor, which has been granted through the love and the Holy Spirit of God and Christ for all people. John's account of Christ's last meal emphasizes strikingly how love works in humility and mutual service: "He loved his own who were in the world . . . to the end" and demonstrated this love by washing his disciples' feet and by telling them to follow his example and do likewise (John 13:1–17).

It may seem cheap and exegetically less than exact to mix the Pauline teaching on the social character of the Lord's Supper with selected quotations from the Gospels. Though Paul himself quotes a text of institution that closely resembles the Synoptic, especially the Lukan, parallel institution texts, his exhortations concerning a decent and a worthy celebration of the meal need not automatically coincide with the witness and intention of the Gospels. I intend now to examine more closely the Gospels of Luke and John, which contain extensive materials concerning Jesus' final supper.

Meals in Luke's Writings

In approximately one-fifth of the sentences in Luke's Gospel and in Acts, meals play a conspicuous role. Events in the life of Jesus and of the Apostles, in the time before and after Easter, and a host of brief sayings and extended parables emphasize the relevance of eating. Like converging rays, the Lukan stories and words about meals are gathered in Luke's account of the Lord's Supper and in his references (in Acts) to the "breaking of the bread." Which character and function, effect and sense, have eating and drinking in the writings of Luke?

(1) Without food, physical life is in danger and, in the long run, impossible. We eat in order to live, as exemplified by the temptation story, the account of the feeding of the multitudes, the petition for daily bread in the Lord's Prayer, and the parable of the Rich Fool. Luke the physician (cf. Col. 4:14) soberly acknowledges that food is indispensable for the sustenance of body and soul. Among the controversial questions are the following. How to get it? What about fasting and gluttony? How much is enough? How wise is it to disregard the imminent crisis, as demonstrated by Noah's contemporaries, who ate and drank in a business-as-usual mood? Does food suffice to still *all* human needs?

(2) Luke is prone to subscribe to what is commonly considered an Epicurean creed: we live in order to eat. Although surprising, this tendency is a fact in Lukan narratives. Peter's mother-in-law, Jairus' daughter, the church sleeper Eutyches, the younger of the prodigal sons, Lazarus in Abraham's lap, and the disciples at Christ's heavenly table are given food *after* they have been saved from disease, death, and all the miseries of the present. By eating together, they celebrate the liberation from physical and spiritual sufferings. Not only temporal but also eternal bliss is depicted as a glorious festival meal.

(3) The presence of the Messiah among the people marks the beginning of a festival time. Actually, his coming is the reason for celebration. In Jesus' presence the disciples are privileged as once David's companions had been: they may eat what others are prohibited from eating. They need not fast as John the Baptist's disciples do.

When Jesus enters the home of Zacchaeus, salvation has come to its inhabitants and to the guests who are present: Jesus eats with them. The common meal with sinners, the feeding of thousands of hungry people, the banquet and dance arranged for the prodigal who has returned home—such events loudly proclaim, "Now is the day of salvation" (2 Cor. 6:2). The day of great joy for all the people (cf., e.g., Luke 2:14; 13:17) has dawned.

(4) By eating and drinking with the disciples between Easter and the ascension, Jesus demonstrates at least three things: he has been raised bodily; he resumes full communion with people who have forsaken him and despaired of the salvation they hoped he would bring; and he equips them to be trustworthy witnesses to his resurrection and to new life, to the life that he has brought to sinners such as they are. The so-called Easter meals are exceptional events, restricted to the forty days between Christ's resurrection and ascension (Acts 1:3–4; 10:40–41). They are identified neither with the "breaking of bread" celebrated in the congregation after Pentecost or during a storm in the belly of a doomed ship nor with the messianic meal to be held in the future world.

(5) The substance of the consumed food rarely or never of itself produces specific effects. Certainly Luke recognizes fully the symbolic value of mother's milk, of wheat that is stored in barns, of bread in the mouth or in baskets, of a fatted calf, and of salt. In Acts 15 the prohibition of the drinking of blood is endorsed; in a vision described in Acts 10 and 11, the problem of whether Christians may eat meat from unclean animals plays a major role. Indeed, Luke records Jesus' warning of the leaven of the Pharisees, and he speaks of the public disgust for people who imbibe too much wine. But his main accent is upon the fact of a given meal rather than upon the substance and quality of the consumed food.

(6) Decisive everywhere is the question, in whose company is a meal held in which one or another food or drink is served. When Jesus is the guest, when he is host, or when he is an invited guest and then turns out to be the real host, the meal held in communion with him is a great and in most cases a salutary event. According to Luke, on two occasions when Jesus sits at the table of publicans and other sinners

and on three occasions when he accepts invitations to the house of a Pharisee, disputes arise over the table. Indeed, upon the all-too-righteous, who resent Jesus' association with the moral outcasts, the common meal brings judgment and condemnation. Thus, at the common table the effect of communion with the Lord, who is Judge and Savior at the same time, is revealed. Unless Jesus is the Lord of the banquet, no festival meal can be truly enjoyed. The promise is given, in the form of a testament, that Christ will let his own people eat and drink with him eternally.

(7) Whoever sits at the table with Jesus must also accept the other guests in Christ's company. Jesus is never without his elect, including especially the outcast. No one can have Jesus for oneself alone; Jesus is met within a strange entourage—the publicans and the sinners, the poor and the bums from the hedges and byways, a notorious woman whom Jesus permitted to touch his feet, the prodigal sons, and such treacherous and cowardly disciples as Judas and Peter and the other disciples who partook of Jesus' last meal (none of whom loved him enough to arrange his funeral). Whoever considers those table companions of Jesus too bad, too base, too little, too far removed from salvation to be met at Jesus' side does not see, accept, and believe Jesus as he really is. Whoever feels too good and too noble to be found in that company cannot sit at the Lord's table. Only when the bums just mentioned have been received and waited upon is Jesus received, and only then does Jesus accept the service rendered to him.

(8) What happens at the common table to those who eat and drink with Jesus, and what are *they* doing? According to Luke's accounts, they eat and drink the natural food that is on the table; they do not consume trans- or consubstantiated miracle substances. They receive a service and eventually render a service to Jesus and the others present. They receive their share and share what they have received. They hear what Jesus and others have to say, and, more often than not, they also speak. Exposed to his talk, they are also engaged in conversation. To eat and drink without talking would be no good; it would contradict the character of the festival meal. From Jesus the people at the table receive information about Jesus and the kingdom of God; also they may come to a better knowledge of themselves.

(9) Finally, love for Jesus does not exclude amazement and holy fear. But often great joy—that the Lord has come and that the lost has been found—expresses the essence and proves to be the result of eating and drinking. The Deuteronomic command "You shall eat before the LORD your God, and you shall rejoice" (Deut. 12:7, 12, 18; 14:26; 27:7) is now fulfilled. According to Didache IX—X, the Lord's Supper is a meal of joy and of thanksgiving, a *eucharist*. In many of Luke's accounts of stories and sayings concerning meals, joy is explicitly mentioned, as in his description of the breaking of bread in Acts 2:46. Translated literally, this verse speaks of "resounding jubilation," i.e., of enthusiastic outbursts.

In substance Luke says the same about the table of Christ that Paul says in 1 Corinthians 10—11, although the difference in style and method is indisputable. Paul, teaching in a doctrinal and liturgical tone, bitterly reproaches the Corinthians for their misuse and for the disorder of the meal. Luke, however, is an artistic storyteller who charms by his way of narration. He records events that set precedents, good and bad examples of conduct, in a way that children as well as sophisticated adults are bound to appreciate. However, the ethical character of eating and drinking with Jesus is pointed out with equal strength by Paul and by Luke. The meal itself is not a mystery or a transfer of salvation. What occurs at the table is a proclamation of Jesus Christ's goodness, of his association with sinners and his full solidarity with them—of all that is most clearly demonstrated in his death on the cross, between two criminals. Love for this Christ can be shown only when the neighbors chosen by Christ are gladly accepted.

If the Lord's Supper has the social and ethical nature I have sketched, then its radiance cannot disappear when the assembly for worship ends. It fills and determines the everyday lives of all who participate.

Festival Time and Everyday Life

Being a neighbor, having neighbors, and eating and drinking with neighbors are not limited to the room or the house in which the Lord's Supper is celebrated. In First Corinthians, Paul's discourses on baptism and the Lord's Supper are interrupted, illustrated, elucidated, and crowned by his general and specific ethical warnings and directives. From Luke we learn that the manifold dimensions of the Supper, which the Lord has instituted, are clearly perceived only when the daily, the occasional, and the festival meals—the meals in which Jesus participated, which he arranged, of which he spoke, and to which he added promises for the eternal future—are kept in mind and used as interpretive keys. The arrangements made at the apostolic council, according to Acts 15, pertain to the Lord's Supper as well as to every daily meal. In Antioch the table community between Christians of Jewish and of Gentile origin was in danger of being broken up because of the legalistic scruples of visitors from Jerusalem. In interpreting Galatians 2:11–14, it is impossible to decide whether the Apostle is speaking of the celebration of the Lord's Supper, of special festival banquets, or of ordinary daily meals. The sermon on justification by the grace and faithfulness of Christ alone, which the Apostle delivered to the segregationists in Antioch, is applicable to any of these occasions. In Acts, when Luke speaks of the breaking of bread and of having all things in common, again it is impossible to say whether he speaks of the Lord's Supper or of the daily use of possessions for charitable, social purposes. Probably he means both. When understood as prolongation, fulfillment, and crowning of the Jewish Passover, the celebration of the Lord's Supper is a cultic action to be celebrated on festival days only. But when we see its function among the many disorders plaguing and dividing the Corinthian congregation and consider all the table scenes and the speeches about eating and drinking in Luke's writings, the Supper is a paradigmatic event among and for practically all daily situations. Probably as early as during Paul's lifetime, *thanksgiving* and *to give thanks* (Greek *eucharistia* and *eucharisteo*) had become terms by which the solemn cultic celebration in the community was described. This usage, though, does not exclude the idea that thanksgiving and praise also belong in daily conduct and are basic to the everyday existence of the congregation and each Christian. This idea is succinctly expressed in Colossians 3:17: "whatever you do, in word or deed, do everything in the name of the Lord Jesus, giving thanks to God the Father through him." When the meaning of "every word" and "every deed" is taken seriously, then every hour, every place, every encounter, and every situation is sanctified and claimed for thanksgiving. Zechariah (14:20) goes as far as to say, "on

that day there shall be inscribed on the bells of the horses, 'Holy to the
LORD.' And the pots in the house of the LORD shall be as the bowls
before the altar." Allegedly secular things and the use of them, together with supposedly secular acts (such as physical eating and drinking) and all that belongs to living in this world, are seized for the praise
of God and for service to God and to one's neighbor. Everything is an
occasion and shall become a means of proclaiming that the crucified
and living Lord rules over the universe now, not only over some souls
in the distant future.

This relationship between the Lord's Supper and everyday life
shows that Christ's table and meal have a social character that is
related to the personal and political lives of all people. No sphere of
life remains unaffected by it. The Supper is a missionary and a social
happening. Either all of Christian ethics is eucharistic—as expounded
in the third section of the Heidelberg Catechism—or Christians have
nothing distinctive to "do in remembrance" of Christ.

It is difficult to describe with one term the relationship between
the festival act of celebrating the Lord's Supper and the daily activities and sufferings of Christians. Is the Supper a school, an exercise, a
training ground, an example to be imitated, a demonstration and display, the criterion and test, the summit of a mountain or a pyramid,
the source that supplies strength and anticipation of the heavenly joys
as final reward? Each of these descriptions may contain a grain of
truth. Accepting and loving one another, especially the little ones,
sharing in earthly goods after God has lavished riches upon us, being a
witness to Christ and being oriented toward his promised Parousia—
such things are indeed exercised and demonstrated by and during the
Supper. However, all pedagogical, mechanical, and potentially legalistic concepts ought to be avoided. May it suffice to say that the Lord's
Supper is a gift of God, which points the way and strengthens us on
our way to loving God by loving our neighbors. In the Lord's Supper
all is ethical; however, only *evangelical* ethics—not legalistic ethics—
fit and express the praise that Christians owe to God and the testimony
that they are to give to each other and to those who do not yet believe
in God as revealed through Jesus Christ and the Holy Spirit.

4

The Witness of John 6

Christ—the One and Only Sacrament

A Striking Countertestimony?

When in a court of law two or three witnesses substantially agree in their testimony and only one witness contradicts them, the verdict will probably be based upon the evidence proffered by the majority. In the preceding chapters it was shown that the New Testament contains two or three convergent testimonies concerning the Lord's Supper. There are two when the Synoptics are grouped with Paul, three when Luke is treated as an independent voice that complements the almost synonymous testimonies of Matthew and Mark. However, the Johannine writings seem to give not only a different but an opposite testimony on all vital issues, that is, concerning the relationship of the eucharist to Jewish worship, the nature of communion with Christ, and the social relationship of the participants in the meal. We have to be open to the possibility that in questions of truth a minority of one may count more than the majority and may even overrule it.

Crucial to my inquiry is John 6, the chapter containing Jesus' speech on food that does not perish (vss. 26–34); on himself, the substance and the giver of the bread of life (vss. 35–51a); and on eating his flesh and drinking his blood (vss. 51b–58). Four times (vss. 54, 56–58) the Greek text surprises the reader by using, instead of the verb *eating* (which occurs eleven times in the whole of John 6), the seemingly crude verb *chewing*. (The RSV always substitutes the nobler *eating*; thus, the biblical text is—in a well-meant but arbitrary way—toned down, so much so that it loses some of its obvious and probably intended bite.) Surprising too is the statement about the uselessness of the flesh and the life-giving power of the Holy Spirit and of the words of Christ (vs. 63), because it seems to contradict what is said in verses 51b–58 about the usefulness of eating the flesh of Christ for eternal life. Also, one may ask whether verse 63 opposes, or invalidates, the glorious affirmation of John 1:14, "The Word became flesh."

Among other pertinent (eucharistic?) texts in Johannine writings are the following: (1) the foot-washing scene in John 13:1–20; (2) the report on blood and water issuing from the crucified Jesus' side after a soldier's lance thrust (19:34–35); (3) the coming of Jesus Christ through and in water and blood, and the testimony of the Spirit (1 John 5:6–8); and (4) the beautiful image of Christ standing and knocking at the door in order to be admitted to a common meal (Rev. 3:20). However, a careful interpretation of these four passages, also of the changing of water into wine at the marriage in Cana (John 2:1–11) and of the image of Christ the Vine (John 15:1–11), would make this book too long (but can be found in the German edition). Because John 6 is the most outstanding of the Johannine texts that might have to do with the Lord's Supper, I wish to concentrate exclusively on some details of this chapter.

I repeat: John seems to contradict flatly the Matthean/Markan, Lukan, and Pauline ways of understanding the Lord's Supper. Contradictions appear in at least three areas.

(1) The fourth Gospel is often believed to express strong antijudaistic sentiments. Is not Jesus here posed against rather than with the Jews? John 8:44 sounds hostile: "You are of your father the devil, and your will is to do your father's desires. He was a murderer from the beginning, and has nothing to do with the truth." The immediate con-

text (8:42–47) and other sharp controversies between Jesus and Jewish speakers in chapters 5 and 7—12 are not the only expressions of harsh judgments upon the Jews. The so-called eucharistic chapter 6 bristles with critical remarks and hints: after a vain attempt to make Jesus their king (vss. 14–15), the Jews fail to see the meaning of the signs that Jesus has given, especially the feeding of the thousands and the walk on the water (vss. 1–25). The Jewish eyewitnesses appreciate only the filling of their stomachs, yet they ask for another sign. Their trust in Moses, who gave Israel's ancestors bread from heaven, prevents them from believing in Jesus Christ (vss. 26–32). They murmur because they presume to know exactly whose son Jesus is (vss. 34, 36, 41–43). They question whether he can give them his flesh to eat (vs. 52). A larger circle of (Jewish) disciples finds Jesus' words hard and offensive (vss. 60–61). The disciples who do not believe in Jesus turn their backs upon him (vss. 64, 66, 67). Even among the chosen Twelve, there is Judas the traitor (vss. 70–71). Specifically insulting is Jesus' repeated assertion that the proudly remembered ancestors of Israel, who were led and fed by God, "ate the manna" in the wilderness and "died" (vss. 49, 58).

Certainly there are counterbalances to a one-sided antijudaistic interpretation of John's Gospel that is built upon a haphazard selection of Johannine texts. Jesus also says, "salvation is from the Jews" (John 4:22), and he speaks of an "Israelite in whom is no guile" (1:47). This Gospel records good things about Nicodemus and Joseph of Arimathea, both of whom were members of the Sanhedrin. Moses does not stand in fundamental contrast to Jesus and to faith in Jesus (1:17; 5:45–47). When Jesus scolds Israel, he follows in the footsteps of good Jews such as Amos, Hosea, Jeremiah, Ezekiel. At all times Jewish self-criticism was harder than anything Gentiles said or could have said against God's own people. The meaning of the term *Jews*, literally *Judeans*, varies within this Gospel. Political and religious authorities, inhabitants of the earlier Southern Kingdom, the madding crowd screaming for Jesus' crucifixion, and other special groups among the children of Abraham are called Judeans. The Jews are depicted as split among themselves (7:43; 9:16; 10:19). Not only "several" but "many" Jews believe in him (8:31; 11:45; 12:11). Jesus is and remains "the King of the Jews," as fixed in writing over the cross by, of all people, the

Gentile Pilate. However, not even these and other pro-Jewish elements negate the crisis that Jesus Christ brings upon Israel.

(2) John creates the impression that eating, drinking, chewing a special food, replaces the proclamation of the Lord's death, which, manifested by love for the poor and weak, is the essence of the Lord's Supper—according to 1 Corinthians 10—11. It seems that a physical consumption of a miraculous medicine—provided the eating and the drinking are inspired by God's Spirit and carried out in faith—takes the place held (esp. in Luke and Paul) by a missionary testimony to Christ crucified. What the other New Testament witnesses have said about the criteria for this testimonial meal, that is, about the participants' loving, mutual acceptance, reciprocal service, and humility, seems in John 6 to be replaced by gross individualism, if not egotism. Is not a blunt physical process—eating and drinking—declared to be the condition of individual salvation? The person who chews and drinks has eternal life and will be resurrected; those who eat and drink remain in Jesus, and Jesus remains in them. Each time, Jesus' words are addressed to individuals. If they fail to eat his flesh and drink his blood, they are excluded from the life that is the possession, privilege, and gift of God and Jesus Christ (6:52–58).

Jesus Christ gives his gift, which is himself (6:51a), directly to each recipient. An easily overlooked difference between John's and the Synoptic writers' accounts of the feeding of the five thousand might confirm this. The fourth Gospel does not mention that the disciples distribute the food to the multitudes; Jesus personally dispensed to each individual the bread and the fish (6:11; unlike Matt. 14:19; 15:36; Mark 6:41; 8:6; Luke 9:16). This christocentric (and perhaps anticlerical) concern is, however, adumbrated by the fact that in John 6:52–58 individualistic, materialistic, and mechanical notions seem to have gained the upper hand. Although communion with Christ is depicted in a most impressive form, this communion seems to take the form of individual gain, without any care for one's neighbors. We might compare it with a miraculous public eating place where food is served free: since anyone who likes the food can go there, the difference between the attending persons does not count. Each one eats simply to fill his or her personal needs.

Again, it may be objected that both at the beginning and at the end of John 6 the community of the twelve disciples, the character and behavior of Jesus' followers, and the acts of some of them are not only mentioned but are constitutive of the events recorded. The disciples' role in the feeding of the thousands, during the crossing of the stormy lake, and in their desperate flight from Jesus, and the report on Peter's confession of faith in Christ form the framework of all that is said about the imperishable food, Jesus Christ, the Bread of Life. Elsewhere in the Gospel of John, especially in chapters 13—16 (and equally in the first and second epistles of John), brotherly love, service, and sharing are the indispensable form, even the criterion, of love for God. But why does John place these chapters relatively far from the discourse on Christ, the True Bread, on the eating and chewing of Christ's flesh, and on the drinking of his blood?

Certainly the counterarguments against an exclusively individualistic interpretation of John 6 cannot dispel the impression that John 6 speaks of a mysterious personal consumption of miraculous food that conveys and guarantees eternal life.

(3) Faith in the sacrament of the meal seems to be the presupposition, the port of entry, the basis, the school, the application, or the criterion of faith in Jesus Christ. Though faith is not mentioned in verses 52–58, the verb *believe* occurs nine times before and after these verses. It is obvious that in verses 29, 30, 35, 36, 40, 47, 64 (twice), and 69 faith *in Christ* is meant and that this faith is inseparable from, even identified with, faith in God, who has sent the Son (e.g., 12:44; 14:1; 17:3, 8). But as Exodus 14:31; 2 Chronicles 20:20 (cf. 1 Chron. 29:20); and John 5:46–47 speak of believing in the Lord *and* in Moses, or in the Lord *and* the prophets, so christocentric and sacramental faith might be described as co-inherent and co-incident in John 6. The theory has been aired, e.g., by Oscar Cullmann, that as early as the time of the writing or the final redaction of the Gospel of John, the christological anti-Docetism was reflected in the sacramental anti-Docetism developed by Ignatius and Justin Martyr. Docetism in Christology denies that the eternal Son and Logos ever became truly human; its sacramental counterpart would not accept that the eternal Christ is physically present in the elements of bread and wine. If John 1:14 and 1 John 4:1–3 refute the christological heresy, then, so it is argued, John 6:51–58 was written to fight a sacramental equivalent. If

this assumption is tenable at all, faith in the sacramental presence of Christ is the condition, shape, and expression of faith in the person of Emmanuel, that is, of God, who is with us in the person of Jesus of Nazareth. The sacrament, in consequence, would be an extension of the incarnation, a miracle and mystery as great as the Logos' becoming flesh at Christmas. On the other hand, none of the approximately ninety occurrences of the verb *believe* (never the noun *faith*) denote belief in a sacrament or a completing of faith in God and the Son by sacramental faith.

Still, it may be asked whether or not the signs done by Jesus according to the fourth Gospel reveal the indispensable role of symbolic actions for faith. Indeed, the signs given by Jesus, which elsewhere in the New Testament are called miracles or mighty deeds, can contribute to evoking faith (2:11, 23; 3:2; 4:53–54; 6:30, 36; 7:31; 9:16; 12:18, 37–42; 20:30–31). But they are not fail-safe instruments (6:2, 14–15, 30, 36; 12:37). The eyes of eyewitnesses have to be opened in a special way, or else the people around Jesus do not make use of their eyes (9:39; 11:40; 12:38–40) and therefore are blind to the recognition marks of the promised Messiah. Although since the days of Augustine, baptism and the Lord's Supper have been called effective signs, in John's Gospel they are not given this name or any other summary title. Neither does this Gospel indicate that they are a quasi-institutional extension of Jesus' acts of healing or resurrecting, of making wine out of water or bread sufficient for thousands out of a few loaves. Toward the end of the Gospel, in 20:29 (cf. 20:30–31), people who believe are blessed—even when they, unlike the Apostles who have been privileged to become eyewitnesses (1:14; 19:35), have not seen Jesus.

Some doubts remain, nevertheless. Does or does not John 6 contain the unique message that faith in Christ cannot exist unless it passes the test of being faith in the mystery of the eucharist? The distinct witness of John 6 may indeed have more weight than the combined testimonies of the other New Testament witnesses. We must face the possibility that John 6 demonstrates the falsity of most or all interpretations of the eucharistic texts I presented in chapters 1—3.

In fact the witness of John 6 is so impressive that, in the course of the church's history, liturgies, and doctrine, the exposition and application of other New Testament texts have always been dominated by the respect paid to John 6. Occasionally the term *breaking of bread*, the emphasis on loving, sharing, serving, the command of human action by the words "do this," or other spiritual and ethical expositions have been used to resist sacramentalistic interpretations. In such instances the social and ethical character of the meal has been placed in the foreground—at the expense of faith in transubstantiation, physical presence, material eating and drinking of divine food. But high sacramental scholars have always seemed to score easily against spiritualizing and ethicizing troublemakers. As soon as they quoted John 6, especially verses 51–58, the stronger biblical arguments seemed to speak in their favor. This is true in three of the four schools of interpretation of John 6 that can be distinguished today. Only the fourth is opposed to a sacramentalistic interpretation.

(1) The first school asserts that verses 32–51a (or 27–51a) must be interpreted spiritually; for this group of theologians the terms *food that endures to eternal life, true bread, bread of life,* and *eat*—except when *eat* refers to the manna consumed in the wilderness—have a symbolic meaning. It is held that the verses use metaphorical diction and speak only of faith in Christ. However, in verses 51b–58 the sacrament of the eucharist is, according to this school, discussed in a rather materialistic way.

(2) The next group of interpreters teaches that the whole passage (vss. 32[or27]–58) bespeaks the sacrament, though at the beginning only food, not drink, is mentioned. Because, however, verse 35 speaks of thirst, not only of hunger, it is assumed that a sacramental drinking complements the eating of the imperishable food, the Bread of Life, and the chewing of Christ's flesh described especially in verses 50–51a and 52–58. A mention of bread and eating without a reference to drinking (vss. 32–35a, 41–51a, 58), then, may not only be an abbreviated form of speech but may also imply permission to distribute and receive the eucharist *sub una* (bread or wafers only, without the distribution of wine to all participants).

(3) If we follow the third school, verses 32–58 have spiritual as well as sacramental meaning; all of them speak of faith in Christ the Bread *and* of the miraculous sacrament. Still a distinction may be made by adherents of this interpretation: in verses 32–51a the spiritual faith in Christ and in verses 51b–58 faith in the symbol, the effective sign,

even the sacrament, bear the main emphasis.

The compromise between schools 1 and 2, which is achieved by school 3, has often been sealed by a summary exegesis of verses 32–58: only in and by and for Christian faith does the sacrament convey life; if there is no faith, God's judgment (described in 1 Cor. 11:27–33) falls upon those who consume the elements, which look and taste like bread and wine but which in reality have become divine substances. According to this exegesis, it is love of the unbelieving neighbor that compels true believers to consider nonsacramentalists "unworthy" persons and to keep them away from the Lord's table.

(4) The fourth school is spearheaded by Augustine, who understands verses 32–58 as a description of the faith relationship to Christ. Although in the exposition of other New Testament texts and in some monographs this church father unfolds high sacramental doctrines, he abstains from such an interpretation in his exposition of John 6. According to Augustine, this whole chapter is an invitation to believe in Jesus Christ. John 6:47 is, then, the core, the summary: "Truly, truly, I say to you, he who believes [in me] has eternal life." Zwingli and Adolf Schlatter, among others, have come to the same conclusion.

Before proceeding in the direction chosen by the fourth group, I wish to mention briefly three ways in which historical-critical scholarship suspects, denigrates, or disparages the fourth Gospel in its totality or the sacramentalist exposition of John 6 as a whole or the supposed sacramentalism found in verses 51b–58.

It is being held that the Gospel of John is the latest of the four canonical Gospels. The earliest date proposed is approximately A.D. 90. Though this Gospel may contain elements as old as, and similar to, the tradition(s) used by Mark (esp. concerning John the Baptist's activity, some miraculous deeds, the disciples, and the Passion), the accounts of Jesus' words are not considered historically reliable. It does seem strange (and is not considered trustworthy) that during his earthly ministry Jesus of Nazareth would always have spoken like the exalted Christ—as it were, from beyond the crucifixion and the resurrection. All too often he makes summary statements on his work, his signs, and his death, as if he were looking back (or down) on them after their completion! His main opponents are no longer the Sadducees but the Pharisees, who in Galilee began to reconstitute and rule Israel only after A.D. 90, that is, more than two decades after the destruction of Jerusalem by the Romans. The formal expulsion from the synagogue (usually called the synagogue-ban, mentioned in John 9:22; 12:42; 16:2) was a defensive measure taken by Pharisees only in that period. The high Christology of the Gospel, including the Wisdom attributes imposed upon Jesus Christ, such as preexistence, mediatorship of creation, and divinity, was a climax reached only after a long development of christological teaching. In the early days of Christianity, Jesus was supposedly hailed only as a rabbi, a prophet, the servant of God, or a similarly outstanding human person, whose death of course contributed to the respect paid to him. If, then, the Gospel was written so late and is historically unreliable, John 6 represents a churchly understanding of the eucharist rather than an expression of Christ's own will, institution, and bequest. Thus is it argued by a large group of historical-critical scholars.

The Gospel of John is assumed not only to reveal acquaintance with pagan, especially Gnostic, myths and allegedly corresponding mystery cults and sacred meals but also to succumb repeatedly to non-Christian thought-patterns. Certainly it is admitted that this Gospel attempts to battle those myths and rituals. It does emphasize the incarnation of the Word as an event in history; it insists upon the scandal of the cross; and it calls for ever-new ethical decision, even for faith and love. All this and more distinguish it from Gnosticism pure and simple. However, it is assumed that in fighting the adversary, the Gospel also has become a victim of foreign religious beliefs and practices that are neither Jewish nor genuinely Christian. Therefore the Gospel is considered a sample of "acute hellenization of Christendom" (Adolf von Harnack's phrase), especially of the doctrines of the Son of God, of salvation, and of worship. Obvious traits of theosophy and mysticism, the concern for the individual human self, and generalizing statements about the world allegedly demonstrate the distance from the teaching of Jesus and of his true disciples. It is freely acknowledged that this Gospel may have contributed to the spread of Christendom throughout the Mediterranean world and the Near East. At the same time, however, through adaptation to religions of the environment, the message of Christ lost some of its originality and (according to Paul, scandalous) strangeness, even its essence. Does not the fourth

Gospel reflect and endorse the gnostic myth of a descending and ascending messenger, sent by the All-Father in heaven and returning to him? Does it not foster a basically dualistic worldview? What does John 6:51–58 imitate except a form of Mithraism, in which unification with the dying and rising deity was sought by a ritual bloodbath and by consuming part of an ox? Finally, does not John's Gospel express the individualistic search for salvation of the soul by a flight out of this world and into heavenly mansions? In endeavoring to underline the difference between Christians and Jews, it is considered no wonder that (e.g., in the discourse on the bread of life and on the eating of Christ in ch. 6) this Gospel emphatically asserts the Jews' lack of understanding, their shock and hurt, the scandal they suffered, and their open hostility and resistance to Jesus. In short it is being held that conditions and disputes of a period *after* the death of Jesus and his Apostles are described in the fourth Gospel.

Literary criticism is convinced that it has discovered four sources from which the present form of the fourth Gospel was composed: (1) a sign-source describing (seven?) miracles done by Jesus; (2) an originally non-Christian gnosticising speech-source that was adapted to church use by additions concerning incarnation, physical death on the cross, and ethical decision; (3) links between narratives and comments contributed by the Evangelist, who created, from the first two primary sources, the Gospel attributed to John; and (4) insertions into the finished work of the Evangelist, so-called interpolations, which are thought to stem from an "ecclesiastical redactor." These insertions mainly pertain to the sacraments of baptism and the eucharist (3:5; 6:51b–58) and to the future resurrection and judgment (e.g., 5:25–29). The additions made the Gospel acceptable and respectable to the majority of churches. Supposedly most congregations had at first refused to use an account of Jesus' life, death, and resurrection that lacked both a report on the institution of the sacraments and an announcement of the future eschatological judgment and resurrection. Once again, the so-called eucharistic passage in John 6 is definitely labeled a product of the postapostolic church, not a reproduction of the words spoken by the historical Jesus.

The consequences of these three attacks upon the authenticity of the crucial verses of John 6 seem obvious. Certainly it is conceded that the sacramental beliefs, liturgies, doctrines, and practices of the post-apostolic and later churches (be they Eastern or Western, Greek or Russian Orthodox, Roman Catholic, Lutheran, Reformed, or of some Free Church types) have a biblical foundation in John 6. However, it is made very plain that their historical age and basis are problematic: they have little or nothing to do with the will and words of Jesus himself, as reconstructed by historical research in the past two hundred and fifty years.

A wholehearted direct attack upon the transformation of baptism and the Lord's Supper into sacraments seemed to be called for; it would have been the logical consequence of the historical insights supposedly gained. A call for *desacramentalization*, comparable to the alleged urgency of *demythologization* of the preached Christ and of the means of salvation (of Christology and soteriology), seemed to be urgently needed. However, with very rare exceptions the sacramental doctrines and practices of the great churches were neither really touched nor challenged nor changed by these "results" of critical scholarship.

Obviously, the arguments used by the critics did not convince the critical scholars themselves, the church leaders, the synods, and the huge majority of church members. Even radical scholars were and are condoning and supporting the existence and ongoing celebration of baptism and eucharist as means of grace, even as sacraments. Whether this acceptance of the status quo is hailed or regretted, it may be useful to ask whether a different interpretation of John 6 is available.

An Alternative Interpretation of the So-Called Eucharistic Verses

In his Tractate on the Gospel of John (XXV.12; XXVI.1, 19; author's translation, from J.-P. Migne, *Patrologia Latina*, vol. 35 [= *Augustini opera omnia*, ch. 3]), Augustine coined sentences such as these: "Do believe—and you have eaten"; "to believe in him—this is to consume the living Bread." Clement of Alexandria and Origen had anticipated the Augustinian interpretation of John 6; later, Zwingli and Luther's Roman Catholic adversary Cajetan, for example, took it up and made it their own. The sacramental understanding of Chrysostom, Gregory of Nyssa, Cyril of Jerusalem, and Cyril of Alexandria, of the mainstream of Scholasticism, and of the Reformation was contradicted at all times. Mainly, it was the great respect shown to Augustine in the West that kept the opposition alive.

However, the earlier mentioned compromise between Augustine's voice in the wilderness and the ubiquitous sacramental practice gained the upper hand. For example, according to Calvin and Luther, Augustine intended to say that the eating during the eucharist had to be done in faith. Thus the opposing parties were sometimes reconciled; the sacramental character of the eucharist was not only safeguarded but also augmented and glorified by reference to the Augustinian position.

Omitting a discussion of how Augustine is or should be truly understood, I turn directly to the biblical text upon which he, as well as his diverse followers and interpreters, grounded his position. One element of John 6:30–58, if seen in the context of the whole Gospel of John, has probably been all too easily neglected in many discussions of this text. Because of this element, critical biblical scholarship may indeed be very useful and can radically and practically influence the celebration of the eucharist in the church.

John's Gospel shows that the form-critical method, which carefully distinguishes various forms of speech and writing, is not an invention of the nineteenth and twentieth centuries. Jesus himself (John 16:25; 18:20), the disciples (16:29; cf. 6:60), the Jews (7:26; 10:24), and the Evangelist (10:6; 11:11, 14) make a distinction between *dark speech*, that is, parabolic, symbolic, figurative speech (called *Bildrede* in German), and *plain talk*. The corresponding Greek terms are *paroimia* and *parrhesia*, respectively. The apocryphal book Ecclesiasticus (39:1–3; 47:17) expresses a common experience of Israel and other nations when it states that it takes a wise person to master the art of interpreting (*hermeneia*) metaphorical or enigmatic discourse. According to the Synoptic Gospels, the meaning of Jesus' parables would sometimes have remained hidden had he not revealed their sense in plain talk. For an understanding of the *Bildreden* (figurative discourses) in the fourth Gospel, it is better to consult the Old Testament and the later Jewish prehistory of the key terms used (such as *shepherd, vine*, and *light*) than to rely on nonbiblical precedents or so-called parallels. If the metaphors used by Jesus can be categorized, they should be called poetic rather than mythological—though the demarcation between the two groups is sometimes hard to draw.

In the fourth Gospel, Jesus often begins a symbolic speech with the words "I am." In his figurative discourses, more than anywhere else, Jesus proclaims who he is and what he does for his people and for the world. When he announces that he is the (Good) Shepherd, the Light (of the world), the Vine (cultivated by God the Father), the True Food, even the Bread of Life, he does not intend to say that he is a personal, physical, or biological specimen among well-known persons and things. Rather he reveals himself as the eternal archetype, a paragon, now descended from heaven (cf. Heb. 8:5; Rom. 5:14; 1 Peter 5:4; Rev. 8:3, 5; 11:19; 21:2).

In the metaphorical speeches in John's Gospel, a second element is almost always present. Imagery, corresponding to the self-revelation of Christ in metaphorical speech, describes the promised and expected deeds and attitudes of the people to whom the Son of God was sent. An anthropological or subjective shell of the *Bildreden* complements the christological or objective core. If Jesus Christ is the Shepherd, the people are the sheep or flock who listen to him, not to a stranger; they follow him and are protected by him from the wolf. Since he is the Vine, they are branches who, when they remain where they belong, are cared for in order to bring forth much fruit. The references to people who eat and are thereby given life correspond to the title "Bread." He who is the Door invites people to enter this door (instead of climbing the fence), and he who is the Way urges them to come and follow him rather than to turn away from him.

The descriptions of the attitudes and actions of the people listening to the revelation of the Messiah's person and work, that is, of the subjective correspondence to the objective gift, are usually as symbolic and figurative as Jesus' self-description. A literal interpretation of the subjective elements of the *Bildreden* would be absurd. Those addressed by Jesus need not bleat "Ba, ba, black sheep" in order to belong to his flock. They are not taught to bathe in sunlight all day long when he calls himself the Light of the world and appeals to them to enjoy the light while it is daytime. Entering through church doors instead of jumping fences makes them as little true Christians, as sitting ("abiding") all night long in a pub called *Zum Rebstock* ("At the Vine"). The figurative, subjective parts of the speeches refer to spiritual, lifelong, existential attitudes and acts, not simply to physical, temporal, external forms of behavior.

In some instances, however, just as in the parables of Jesus recorded in the Synoptic Gospels, the poetic-symbolic speech includes words and phrases that interpret the imagery in plain talk and even refer to physical events and actions. The Good Shepherd actually dies, though not torn to pieces by a wolf, but suspended on the cross, for the sins of the world. When Jesus speaks for himself during his ministry and through his messengers after his ascension, his words are physically heard. To enter his corral will indeed mean to join one of the congregations assembling in Jesus' name for worship. Those who follow Jesus are those who choose one way and reject many others in their daily conduct. *Seeing* can have a metaphoric as well as a physical sense. Still, these traces of plain speech in the symbolic discourse do not mean that the subjective elements must signify exclusively physical actions.

These observations must be applied to the exposition of John 6:51b–58. Taken as plain talk, bare of imagery and figurative significance, these verses would say that either cannibalism or theophagy (eating the deity in the form in which it presents itself, for instance, in a bull) are preconditions, the exclusive means of attaining eternal life. Indeed, every sincere Bible reader must be perplexed, nonplussed, and scandalized by the "hard speech" delivered by Jesus (6:60), especially the words about using his flesh and blood for food. We owe gratitude to the Evangelist for mentioning the Jewish listeners' reaction to Jesus. If we read the words literally, our reaction would be just like theirs. The Bible student who is so blind, dumb, insensitive, and hard-hearted as to sense nothing behind the bare words of John 6:51b–58 would indeed understand nothing. Who could comprehend what Jesus may have meant? Who would not be inclined to murmur? Who would not ponder and perhaps decide to do as the greater part of a large circle of disciples did, that is, to quit Jesus' company (cf. 6:60–61, 66–67; cf. 6:41, 43)? After all, what good could come of chewing up a person or a god, and drinking the blood—together with, or instead of, plain bread and wine?

An alternative does exist to this misunderstanding, this scandalization, which resulted in turning away from Jesus. In modern scholarship it is seldom disputed that in the discourse on the bread of life, *bread* and *eating* are metaphors that (when they are combined) denote two things or events: the gift of God (or of the Son, who gives himself) as the objective element, and the reception and use of that gift by believing people as the subjective element. Most likely verses 51b–58 too—inexplicable as they are when understood as plain, not figurative, speech—are phrased in symbolic diction. If so, flesh and blood, eating, chewing, and drinking are elements of a coherent imagery. As a resumption of the preceding parabolic discourse containing the metaphors *bread* and *eating*, the imagery of verses 51b–58 clarifies the image of bread given and eaten. Instead of explaining the figurative talk of verses 32–51a in plain language, Jesus uses in John 6:51b–58 a combination of metaphors. Interpreting a parabolic speech of Jesus by another speech of Jesus corresponds to the parable explanations in the Synoptic Gospels. However, in John 6, imagery is explained by imagery, one figurative speech by another. Verses 51–58 expand and deepen, illustrate and clarify, the intention of discourse on the bread. This means that both parts of John 6:32–58 have to be understood metaphorically, or else a nonsymbolic reading of verses 51b–58 will lead to the misunderstandings exemplified by the Jewish objection "How can this man give us his flesh to eat?" (6:52). In fact the parabolic diction of these verses *must* be explained as figurative speech that consists of a combination of metaphors. To neglect the metaphorical character of the diction of John 6:53–58 would mean to disregard the literal meaning of these verses—which in this case is figurative—and to contradict the sense that the speaker or writer intended. What, then, is gained by the progress and the transition from the first figurative speech to the second, from verses 32–51a to verses 51b–58?

The bread that the Son gives is explained by "his flesh" and "his blood." Thus the question "How is Jesus the bread of life that can be eaten?" is answered by the statement "Because he became and is flesh and blood, which can be eaten, chewed, and drunk." A reference to Christ's flesh alone could lead to thoughts of incarnation, as the traditional interpretation of John 1:14 and the repeated references to Christ's descent from heaven in 6:33–58 suggest. But I have shown that *flesh* and *blood* mentioned in separate but closely joined verses and poured-out blood (presupposed or explicitly mentioned) refer to the violent death of a person or an animal or the sacrificial death of a lamb, goat, heifer, or ox. Applied to John 6 this means that only by his death is Jesus the Bread of Life; that is, only by giving away his life does he give eternal life to others. This corresponds to the image of the Good Shepherd in John 10: by giving his life in the battle against the wolf, Jesus saves his flock. It is also reminiscent of Jesus' saying about the wheat in John 12:24: only when it falls underground and dies (according to the biological insights prevalent in Jesus' time) can it bring forth fruit. The light of the world pours itself out into the darkness, and by confronting the darkness it gives light. Light is the only salvation, even in darkness.

Although this may explain the objective part of the imagery used in John 6:52–58, even Jesus' proclamation of his sacrificial death, it does not yet explain the corresponding subjective element, the people's response, that is, the mention of eating flesh and drinking blood. It cannot be demonstrated that these terms stem only from the Mithras or another pagan cult. At the banquets Paul mentioned (1 Cor. 10:19–21) perhaps not only was sacrificial meat eaten but also sacrificial blood was consumed, in one form or another. But the fourth Gospel is hardly proclaiming the mystery of the eucharist by endorsing, at least in principle, the bloody part of feasts and sacrifices to idols. The Bible contains two kinds of references in which the eating of flesh and the drinking of blood play a decisive role.

(1) To a sacrificial meal of the end time, which will take place on the mountain of Israel, God invites, or compels, the birds of the air and all the animals of the field. There they shall eat the flesh and drink the blood—not of the usually consumed rams and lambs, goats and bulls and fatted Bashan cows, but of "mighty men," "all kinds of warriors," and "the princes of the earth" (Ezek. 39:17–20). In short, the victory over Israel's enemies is to be celebrated by a ghastly meal in which human beings are devoured and their blood is gulped. The same imagery recurs in the New Testament: in Revelation 16:6; 17:6, 16; and 19:17–18 the victory that enemies have seemingly gained over the members of the church is celebrated in festival demonstrations and actions; the reputed victors eat the flesh or drink the Christians' blood.

Obviously, heinous celebrations of this kind cannot have provided the background for the imagery used in John 6:51–58. Jesus has overcome the world, not vice versa; his, not the world's victory is celebrated; the disciples, not the enemies, hold the feast. It is good to know that another festival type of meal exists, one that bears no trace of cannibalism. This other type forms the background and clearly illustrates the figurative speech found in the enigmatic verses John 6:51–58.

(2) According to prescriptions concerning Old Testament sacrifices, in specific cases, after the cultic slaughtering, not only the priest but also those who have brought the sacrificial animal are given a share of the sacrificial meat to eat. In contradistinction to Canaanite cults, however, those who have brought the sacrifice are strictly prohibited from drinking the blood of the victims. Under all circumstances, the consumption of flesh in which there still is blood is prohibited (Gen. 9:4; Lev. 3:17; 7:27; 17:10–14; Deut. 12:23; cf. 1 Sam 14:33). Only one reason, if any, is given for this restriction: for the life is (in) the blood, or the blood is the life. This prohibition about blood fights at least two ideas: (a) that through the eating of meat, even through a sacrifice and a sacrificial meal, the life of an animal (more or less identified with the re-presented power of a deity) is transferred to the worshiper; and (b) that the life given by God and through the Holy Spirit alone could be attained and secured through cultic actions performed by the worshiper. God reserves the giving, the sustenance, and the salvation of life.

In John 6:52–58 Christ reveals himself as a sacrifice; he completes the imagery of *flesh* and *blood* by speaking of a sacrificial meal in which flesh and blood are consumed. By this figurative speech he conveys a clear message: the life withheld during the time of Old Testament sacrifices is now available, given, and received in his own sacrifice. Nowhere except in his death is the life of Jesus and of God communicated.

The epistle to the Hebrews (chs. 7—10) speaks, though using other words, about the difference between Israel's sacrifices and the sacrificial death of Jesus Christ. John 6:51–58 cannot be separated from all that is said in the New Testament about the uniqueness or completeness of the salvation brought by the Messiah of Israel and the Savior of the world. Also, the Johannine verses do not contribute a new element to other biblical statements about the total and exclusive salvation through Christ crucified. Only the imagery that is used in John's Gospel is unique. The same is true of John 19:34: the water (of life!) and the blood (to be drunk as the carrier of life) flow out of the body of Christ crucified. He who has died on the cross is the source of the life-giving water (which is equated with the Spirit in John 7:38–39 and which flows simultaneously with the life-element blood from the opened side of Christ). Christ alone is the source of the life-conveying food and drink, as well as the food and drink itself. Christ is life itself. Therefore, it is not one or another of the church sacraments to which the gift, the salvation, or the protection of eternal life ought to be attributed.

The obnoxious term *chewing* (*trogein* in John 6:54, 56, 57, 58) can, but need not, mean forceful and noisy chewing or the meditative way in which a cow eats grass and regurgitates. *Chewing* was hardly chosen in order to fight a docetic conception of the sacraments that might have made an issue of the absence or the presence of either heavenly or earthly substances in water, bread, and wine. We have no evidence of groups who combined docetic christological with sacramental beliefs in the late first century or earlier. Rather, according to complete Greek dictionaries, *to chew* often means "to eat with joy and pleasure." This was the proper way to eat when a choice extra dish, such as one prepared with almonds or raisins, was served during or after a meal. *Chewing* probably alludes to the kind of eating, drinking, and rejoicing to which Deuteronomy 12:7, 12 invites. The banquet arranged for the prodigal son after his return (Luke 15:23–27) and the jubilation belonging to the early Christians' breaking of bread (Acts 2:46) illustrate this joy.

In summary it is probable that John 6:51–58 (thus, the whole of John 6) speaks of the incarnation and the sacrifice of Christ rather than of the eucharist. Jesus Christ is praised. For this praise a glorification of sacramental mediation of grace cannot substitute. Verses 51–58 are *eucharistic* only in the sense that they provide ample reason to give thanks to God and to live a life of gratitude. It is fitting and appropriate to read these verses, among other texts, during the Lord's Supper: at this meal Christ crucified is remembered, proclaimed, and praised. However, real thanksgiving is directed to God, through Jesus

Christ (cf. Col. 1:12–14; 3:17), rather than to an honorable form of church worship. No one and nothing deserve a share of the glory that is due the Lamb and God, as the book of Revelation does not tire of repeating. Total faith in God and Jesus Christ is the proper response, and thanksgiving is, as Colossians 3:17 states, the substance of the Christian's every word and deed, not only of the celebration of the Lord's Supper.

John 6:63

Between the eucharistic verses 51–58, which proclaim Christ's death, and the verses 66–71 describing the actions of defective and of faithful disciples, Christ's ascent and return to God in heaven is mentioned (vs. 62). In the speeches about the bread of life and the flesh and blood of Christ, only Christ's delegation by God and his descent from heaven are focused upon (see vss. 33, 38–39, 41–42, 50–51, 58). In verses 30–51a and 51b–58 Jesus' power to resurrect the dead on a future day is repeatedly mentioned (vss. 39, 40, 44, 54). But now that eschatological perspective is, at least in part, presupposed as fulfilled. Verses 62 and 63 speak distinctly to the time *after* Jesus' death and resurrection: "what if you were to see the Son of man ascending where he was before?" (vs. 62). Especially verse 63 is often quoted in monographs on the Lord's Supper:

a: It is the Spirit that gives life,

b: the flesh is of no avail;

c: the words that I have spoken to you, are spirit and life.

In using *life-giving* (*zoopoioun*) to describe the Holy Spirit, line a above summarizes (just as in Rom. 8:11; 1 Cor. 15:45; 2 Cor. 3:6; cf. 1 Peter 3:18) all that is said in the Old and New Testaments about the work of the promised Spirit. The Holy Spirit is God's power to create and renew human beings and all nations; it inspires judges, prophets, and kings; it gathers and reconstitutes Israel from the Exile; it creates Jesus in the Virgin Mary's womb and inspires him from his baptism to the hour of his death; it makes Jesus and his disciples speak about the mighty works of God; it gives them the power to heal the sick and to expel demons; it creates the church at Pentecost; it gives faith, love, hope, and diverse gifts of grace to the members of the congregation; it inspires and maintains unity; it transforms the mortal bodies in the resurrection. Because God's Spirit is to be poured out over all flesh (cf. Joel 2:28 [3:1 in the Hebrew Bible]), it is not in principle opposed to flesh and does not exclude contact with debased humanity. The Spirit goes as far as to regenerate and renew, resurrect and transform miserable human beings. When the Bible affirms that the same Lord creates, reconciles, and redeems heaven and earth, soul and body, it excludes the polytheistic and dualistic mutual exclusion of spirit (or reason) and matter. Yet in John 6:63b, the flesh is totally condemned. The words of Jesus recorded in John 3:6 and 8:15 have the same effect: birth from the flesh and judgments according to the flesh are no good. When *flesh* and *Spirit* are mentioned in the same context (e.g., Ezek. 37; Rom. 1:3-4; 8:5-14; Gal. 5:16-25; 6:8; 1 Cor. 15:42-50; 1 Peter 3:18; 1 Tim. 3:16), the limitation, futility, or corruption of flesh is always presupposed or proclaimed. Creatureliness, confinement by death, dependence on forces outside ourselves for the sustenance of life itself—these features of flesh are not bad in themselves; even they are created and sustained by God. But when "all flesh had corrupted their way on the earth" (Gen. 6:12), flesh fell under God's judgment. When compared with God's Spirit, the flesh is, as John 6:63 aptly sums up the available evidence, "of no avail." In Paul's letters the same effect of God's judgment upon the corrupt flesh is frequently emphasized.

According to part c of John 6:63 both the Holy Spirit and the words of Jesus Christ are the tools that God uses to give life. The two instruments are more or less identified in, e.g., Isaiah 11:4 ("the rod of his mouth," a poetic synonym of "the breath of his lips") and Ephesians 6:17 ("take the sword of the Spirit which is the word of God"). There are two biblical ways to describe the relationship between the Word and the Spirit of God: the Word is the instrument of the Spirit, and the Spirit is the power of the Word (cf. John 20:22-23; 1 Cor. 2:4; Rom. 1:16). The emphatic form of the pronoun *I* (*ego*), used in John 6:63c, shows a distinction between Jesus' words and the words of life spoken by Moses in the law (Deut. 8:3; 30:19-20; 32:47; cf. Acts 7:38), by the prophets, and by later Jewish teachers. However, according to John 1:17; 5:39, 46-47; and 6:32, this differentiation does not exclude the idea that Moses, the law, the Scriptures, the preservation of Israel

in the wilderness, were preparations, indications, and testimonies to
the grace and truth that have been finally brought and revealed
through Jesus Christ.

What is the meaning of the whole of John 6:63? And how does this
verse help us understand the main message of John 6—that Jesus
Christ is the Bread of Life, even through his death? Three main interpretations can be distinguished in scholarly commentaries.

(1) The *sacramental* exposition maintains that the text describes
how the bread and the wine are transformed into the flesh and blood
of Christ: the Holy Spirit must come into action (for this the so-called
epiclesis asks), and the right words must be spoken (as the *forma
sacramenti*, to use the phrase of the Roman Catholic tradition). Some
theologians (among them, Rudolf Schnackenburg) go even further,
saying that this verse indicates more than the transformation of bread
and wine into flesh and blood. They believe that it requires a
distinction between Jesus' earthly and Jesus' heavenly flesh and blood.
They are convinced that only the heavenly, spiritual flesh and blood
are offered, eaten, chewed, and drunk during the eucharist. Thus, the
idea of eating the flesh and drinking the blood of the earthly Jesus of
Nazareth is excluded, and anything resembling cannibalism is
avoided, though the notion of theophagy (consuming the deity or at
least one element of it) is not completely banned. It may be helpful to
recall at this point the traditional sacramental understanding of
"spiritual food . . . and drink" in 1 Corinthians 10:3–4—which I have
not endorsed in discussing the partly obscure verses in 1 Corinthians
10.

(2) In the *anthropological* school of interpretation, two main sub-
groups complement each other. The first concentrates upon the *her-
menuetical* meaning of John 6:63: in John's, as well as in Paul's and
Luke's, writings, the Spirit and the Word are indispensable for
hearing, comprehending, believing, and confessing the message and
the mighty deeds of God. The useless flesh mentioned in John 6:63b is
then human reason and rhetoric, which cannot grasp, encompass, express, or please God—unless God sends the Holy Spirit, which opens
the ear, the heart, and the mouth (and which also inspires the writing
down of things pertaining to God's revelation; cf. 1 Cor. 2:7–16; 2
Tim. 3:16–17). The other subgroup of scholars argues on a *soterio-*

logical level. How is a person saved? John 6:63 answers that one is saved, not by "works of the flesh" (in Pauline terminology, also called "works of law"), but by the fruit of the Holy Spirit (cf. Gal. 5:16–25). Indeed, in John 6:63 the references to the Spirit and to the words of Jesus show that in order to live, a person has to be totally renewed. What people are by nature and what they do mentally, emotionally, functionally, operatively, in short, existentially—all this is flesh and of absolutely "no avail." What they need, what alone can save them, is rebirth by the words and the Spirit of the resurrected Lord (cf. John 3:3–15; 1 Peter 1:3; James 1:18; Titus 3:5). In summary, the second school teaches that salvation from spiritual death, mental blindness, and hopelessness is the gist of John 6:63. No one becomes a true disciple in the sense of John 6:60–69 except through the operation of God's Word and Spirit.

(3) According to a third school the sense of the statements on the quickening Spirit and the useless flesh is *christological*. It is held that the words and the way of the historic Jesus, including his death, would be useless unless this Jesus were, through God's Spirit, raised from the dead and transformed through the preached Word into the "Christ of faith." Silently or explicitly some scholars insert the word *only* (or its equivalent, *exclusively*) in line b of verse 63: if we were given *only* the flesh of Christ (i.e., his way and work in history) and if this way and work were considered exclusively on the level of mortal, corruptible, or corrupted flesh, separated from the operation of the Holy Spirit, then the historic Jesus would be of no avail. This interpretation might, yet need not, bring into question the glorious role ascribed to the flesh in John 1:14: "the Word became flesh and dwelt among us, full of grace and truth; we have beheld his glory." In fact, John 6:63 may emphasize that the Logos' (the Son's) becoming flesh in history was complemented by the work of the Holy Spirit, which raised the crucified Jesus from the dead and which was promised and given to the disciples so that they were enabled to understand and proclaim Jesus' words. Christological confessions (e.g., Rom. 1:3–4; 8:3–4; 1 Tim. 3:16; 1 Peter 3:18) distinguish Jesus Christ "in the flesh" and Jesus Christ "in the Spirit." According to the Gethsemane words recorded in Matthew 26:41 the difference between strong and weak is rooted in the contrast between the Spirit and the flesh. If Jesus Christ were *only* weak, he

would be of no avail. But through the gift and operation of the Word and the Holy Spirit, he is strong, effective, and of singular avail.

The first of the three interpretations is problematic because no other Johannine or New Testament text supports it. It reduces the function of the Word and the Spirit to a technical, though miraculous, transformation of earthly elements. It is difficult to choose between the two other mainstream expositions. Each has biblical parallels and support. A daring combination of the three ways might argue: (1) the mystery of Jesus Christ's own spiritual strength and fleshly weakness (2) is communicated to the church people after Easter through the sacramental transformation of bread and wine (3) and effects liberation *from* deadly works and religious blindness and *to* a new life in the community of believers. However, this ingenious combination would mean that under Christ, the head of the church, the sacrament is the specific and exclusive means of God's communication with humanity. Christ, then, would be reduced to the role of the founder of the sacrament, and only the sacrament would effectively convey the salvation of sinners. The eucharist would in fact take the place that in all biblical writings is reserved for Jesus Christ. Again, an alternative is needed.

In its present context, John 6:63 stands in close relationship to the preceding discourses on Christ's incarnation and sacrificial death, specifically to Christ's ascension, mentioned in verse 62. It also pertains to the subsequent parts of John 6, i.e., to the statements about false and true discipleship. In his confession of faith (vss. 68–69) Peter alludes to the life-giving words of Jesus mentioned in verse 63. Verses 62–63 probably form a bridge between the substance of the speeches on bread, flesh, and blood, on one hand, and the accounts on words, events, and deeds related to discipleship, on the other. In fact verse 63 answers the question, "How is the completed work of Christ (John 19:30), the treasury acquired and gained by his passion, death, and resurrection, prevented from being hidden, unknown, and ineffective?" In his Larger Catechism (in the interpretation of the third article of the Apostles' Creed, section 38) Luther faced this question. His answer is that if no one knew of the treasure in Christ's work and thus no one applied it to himself or herself and enjoyed the use of it, the completed work would be in vain and the treasure lost. To forestall such total loss, "God caused his Word to go out and to be proclaimed whereby he gave the Holy Spirit so as to bring the treasure of redemption home and to appropriate it to us" (author's translation of the German original as printed in *Die Bekenntnisschriften der evangelisch-lutherischen Kirche*, vol. II, Berlin, 1930, p. 654).

In less picturesque but more modern terminology, this means that the application and distribution of the perfect work of God to people, at times and places removed from immediate contact with Jesus of Nazareth, is made through the Word and the Holy Spirit. The problems of bridging the "nasty [or ugly] gap" between then and now (of which Gotthold Ephraim Lessing spoke in the eighteenth century), of the establishment of a direct and firm connection between the unique and the universal, of the communication between Christ, who is one, and us, who are many, are met and solved by God. How does God accomplish it? By clergy and sacraments? John 6:63 answers, by Christ's words and by the Spirit. Word and Spirit form the double powerline or lifeline demonstrating that objectively we humans are included in Christ's work and that subjectively we are drawn into it in order to enjoy its effects. Since God's own *means of grace* are the Word and the Spirit, in the time after Christ's ascension, baptism and the Lord's Supper should no longer be called means of grace. Does this mean the total exclusion or condemnation of everything called sacrament and celebrated as such?

The One and Only Sacrament

If any New Testament book offers good reasons to speak of a *visible word*, an *effective sign* (i.e., an act simultaneously *significative and effective*), a *gift of God*, perhaps even *means of grace*, it is the fourth Gospel. All these terms, including *mystery* (which is never used in the Gospel or the epistles of John), stem from the liturgy and theology of the postapostolic church. They have been coined to define the essence of the sacraments administered by the church. Other mainstreams of the Johannine message notwithstanding, the Gospel of John is centered in and owes its impact much more to its thoroughgoing testimony to the lowly yet exalted, the rejected yet believed, Christ (that is, to its Christology), than to its occasional references to baptism and common meals. Only a forced interpretation would consider every mention of water or wine, eating and drinking, giving or taking, to be an indication that baptism and eucharist are discussed on practically every page of the Gospel.

Actually the quoted ecclesiastical and dogmatic terms are appropriate, if for anything, only for descriptions of Jesus Christ alone. When the word *mystery* is used in the singular in Ephesians and Colossians, it designates Jesus Christ, especially Christ's revelation and performance in joining the Jews and the Gentiles into one people, which is the result of Christ's death and resurrection. According to John 1:14, God's glory is seen in the incarnate Word. The *signs* given by Jesus and recorded in this Gospel are not just traffic signals that tell people whether they should stop or go. Rather, they make certain things and people stop, and they make others go. The great gift of God, in which all other gifts are included (cf. Rom. 8:32), is Jesus Christ (John 3:16; 6:32; 16). In Christ alone are grace and truth incorporated and distributed (John 1:14, 17). Therefore, if the nonbiblical term *sacrament* is to be used at all, a careful interpreter of John's Gospel has to reserve it for Jesus Christ. There is no other mediator, no other means, no other instrument, besides the Son of God and his death for sinners.

In the early years of the Reformation, Luther knew and said this. In commenting on Hebrews 2:3 and 10:19 in his *Commentariolus in epistolam divi Pauli ad Hebraeos* (a series of lectures held in 1517–1518; see the Weimar ed., vol. 57, 1939, pp. 114, 222), Luther insisted on using the term *sacrament* exclusively for the death of Christ. He argued that the cross alone is simultaneously the sign, cause, instrument, and means of salvation. And in his "Disputation regarding Infused and Acquired Faith" (a collection of twenty propositions for a faculty examination in Wittenberg in February 1520), he stated, "In the Holy Scriptures none of the seven sacraments is designated by the name 'sacrament.' The Holy Scriptures contain one sacrament only which is the Lord Jesus Christ himself" (author's translation from the Weimar ed. of Luther's works, vol. 6, 1888, p. 86; cf. p. 97). Later, Luther seemed to have forgotten what he had affirmed earlier. However, among others, Eberhard Jüngel (in *Evangelische Theologie*, vol. 26, 1966, pp. 320–336, esp. pp. 334–336), following hints given by Karl Barth in the later volumes of his *Church*

Dogmatics, revived Luther's thesis in calling Jesus Christ the one sacrament of the church. According to Jüngel, baptism and the eucharist are celebrations of this one sacrament of the church. Recent Roman Catholic theologians (such as Edward Schillebeeckx) have made the following distinctions: Christ is the *Ursakrament* of redemption; the church is the *Allsakrament*; and the several *Sakramente* celebrated in the churches are unfoldings of the *Ursakrament*.

Martin Buber used the term *sacrament* to denote the special dignity and relevance of dialogue and of Israel. I have heard Paul Tillich declare in a discussion that "every element is a virtual sacrament." But it makes little sense to splash the term *sacrament* around too liberally. Rather, we need to look for its purification by a christological concentration.

The ecumenical variety and the traces of harmony among some of the theologians I have mentioned may well demonstrate that the interpretation of the Lord's Supper that I have presented is not typically Calvinist, Reformed, or Presbyterian. Rather, the convergence—as far as it is christocentric rather than centrifugal—shows that, perhaps, as a result of renewed Bible study, the liturgy and the celebration of the Lord's Supper may someday be so reformed as to embrace and unify all Christian churches. The One Shepherd of the one flock invites all people to give thanks to God at one table.

Epilogue

BEM: Questions and Considerations

After working intensively for over almost two years with the Lima documents of 1982 (in the following, called BEM) and some of the consequent secondary literature, I present for discussion some provisional results of my observations and impressions. They can be expressed in the form of four critical questions, which deal with the relationships between: (1) the Word of God and the church, (2) God's accomplished work and the church's sacraments, (3) the celebration of the eucharist and the ordained ministry, and (4) the present scandalous division and the hoped-for future unity of the churches. Each question will be followed by some brief considerations.

I

Does BEM really mean to propose that the independent existence of the church, that is, the structures and traditions, doctrines and practices which stem from the ancient church and later developments, occupy the same rank as (or even in practice a higher rank than) the living Word of God, the con-

stantly renewed listening to that Word, and the ever renewed reformation of the church through the same Word?

Reformed doctrine is not the first nor the only voice to speak of the church as *creatura verbi* (creature of the Word). And yet a prominent Reformed theologian, who contributed much to the production of BEM, seems properly to interpret the intention and results of the so-called "ecumenical convergence" when he writes, "the Church is not constantly being reborn of the Word alone" (*Ecumenical Perspectives on Baptism, Eucharist, and Ministry*, ed. M. Thurian [Geneva: WCC, 1983], p. 8). That an ontology of the church, or a doctrinal and liturgical tradition together with a ministerial succession, participates in the same authority and is entitled to claim the same pious respect as the Word of God witnessed to in Scripture is a notion that belongs, to be sure, to the self-understanding of some three-quarters of the churches represented in the development of BEM. But if such a view were to become a presupposition of the promised and longed for unity of the church and of the proposed "common expression of the apostolic faith today" (BEM, p. x), the result would be only a Three-Quarter Oekumene. This would come to pass only by excluding churches of the Reformed and some Free Church traditions. The division among the churches would only be exacerbated by such a prostration before an institutional Great Church.

To be sure, biblical texts are often referred to explicitly or implicitly in BEM, but in decisive passages on the ministry they are conspicuously absent or meager. Very often in the discussion of baptism and eucharist such biblical texts are adduced which, while they have been used as pillars in liturgical developments and sacramental doctrines since the second century, nevertheless do not speak explicitly of baptism or Lord's Supper at all. For example, John 3:5; 1 Corinthians 6:11; and Hebrews 10:22 are cited to show that baptism effects rebirth, justification, and cleansing of the heart (*Bapt.* 2, 4), while Romans 12:1 and 1 Peter 2:5 are taken to show that our sacrifice is united with Christ's sacrifice in the eucharistic anamnesis (rather vague in *Euch.* 10, clearer in the *Lima Liturgy* 23–24, and clearest in *Ecumenical Perspectives*, pp. 91, 231). It is, then, through the misuse of biblical texts in this fashion that justification, the gift of the Spirit, and baptism are declared to be simultaneous if not identical events (*Bapt.* 7, 8, 10,

14) and that the eucharist is sometimes characterized as a sacrifice
offered by the church which actualizes the sacrifice of Jesus Christ.

II

*Does BEM not give the impression that God's accom-
plished work—the incarnation of Jesus Christ, his death and
resurrection, and the outpouring of the Holy Spirit—would be
ineffective if it were not actualized through baptism, eucharist, and ministry; that is, ontologically mediated, noetically
guaranteed, and thus functionally validated? Does not the
one Mediator and his completed work thereby become dependent on "means of grace," on which the church thinks to have
an administrative monopoly?*

While BEM very impressively recognizes the once-for-all quality
of the sacrificial and liberating death of Jesus Christ and its significance for the salvation of all humanity (*Euch.* 5, 6, 8), it also presents
impressive lists which specify the effects of the sacraments (esp. *Bapt.*
2–4, 14; *Euch.* 1–2, 8, 13–14). Baptism and eucharist are quite properly called gifts of God, but BEM appears to stipulate that through
them alone are mediated and applied God's paramount gifts, that is,
the Son and the Spirit, grace and life, justification and sanctification. It
is, for example, maintained that a person is reborn, incorporated into
Christ, filled with the Spirit, made a new creature, assured of eternal
life, only when confronted with the Christ present in unique fashion
in bread and wine (*Euch.* 13–14). In agreement with almost all pre-
vailing doctrines of the sacraments, it is repeatedly pointed out that
the sacraments signify what they effect and effect what they signify.

It must be admitted that the section on baptism does not explicitly
assert that salvation and the Spirit are given solely through baptism.
Nevertheless, there is ascribed to the eucharist a unique presence of
Christ, a very specific operation of the Spirit, a validation of the sacrifice on the cross, and a particularly effective anticipation of the return
of the Lord. This observation does not mean to deny, of course, that
baptism and eucharist have a necessary and exemplary function for all
true liturgical and ethical service of God.

In the Bible, particularly in the narratives of Acts, water baptism is
always carefully distinguished from Spirit baptism (differing from

Bapt. 14). No eucharistic text whatsoever speaks of an extension of the incarnation, a combination of the sacrifice of Christ with the sacrifice of Christians, or a return of the Lord occurring in the transformed elements of bread and wine. Of course, the authors of BEM do not intend to degrade Christ to a mere founder of the holy sacraments, or the Holy Spirit to a mere instrument of sacramental miracle working. But they say so many and such powerful things in praise of the sacraments that one would almost think that the perfection, validity, and glory of the work of Christ needs ecclesiastical assistance in order to be effective. Because in similar fashion the Holy Spirit is, so to speak, channeled and ritually tamed, also the sovereignty and freedom of the Spirit seem more than merely curtailed; in any case, they are not praised enough.

When the *Lima Liturgy* (22) takes up a variation of the jubilant cry from 1 Timothy 3:16, "Great is the mystery of faith!", it probably does not relate it, as does the biblical text, to Jesus Christ himself. The newly created liturgical context makes the worshiper think rather of an actualization achieved through the miraculous transformation of bread and wine. Long ago, Jeremiah castigated with the strongest possible words a devotion to the temple and the cult of the Lord which blossomed at the expense of worship in spirit and in truth.

III

Does BEM really want to teach that the sacraments are only completely valid when they are celebrated by an official who has been consecrated by episcopal laying on of hands? Is then a hierarchical church structure, especially the distinction between clergy and laity, a precondition for the reception and effectiveness of the gifts of God?

While BEM (*Bapt.* 22) provides for emergency baptism by a non-ordained person, the celebration of the Lord's Supper without the presence of a consecrated priestly official is excluded. While the overall category "ministry" might allow one to consider the presider of the eucharist to be a "servant," other terms point in a direction which does not exclude power, domination, and a claim to monopoly. Jesus spoke very clearly against such claims in Matthew 20:25–26. But the Ministry section of BEM is as long as the Baptism and Eucharist parts put together, and it has the last word. The rendition of "ministry" by *Amt* (office) in the official German version augments the impression that BEM understands the church as a power structure in the sense repudiated, among others, by Luther's *On the Babylonian Captivity of the Church* and by Leonardo Boff in his recent book, *Church, Charism, and Power (1985)*.

Why was the theme of ministry, that is, of ordained clergy, awarded so much space and weight? It is probably because the mutual nonrecognition of church offices and officers contributes more to the separation of the churches than the divergent ways of understanding the sacraments. It must be admitted that the authors of BEM did not want to solve the existing problems by propagating a secular concept of order and power. When they placed the sections on the sacraments before and above the discussion of offices, they hoped to make sure that the celebration of baptism and eucharist, as instituted by Jesus Christ, rather than any given concept of office, is the criterion and means to reunite the divided church. Although these reasons deserve to be taken seriously, some biblical considerations are more important.

In the New Testament, baptism, eucharist, and ministry are never found combined as a triple star in heaven or as three supports of a platform on the earth. While in BEM (*Min.* 11–12, 14, 17) ordained ministers are interpolated as intermediaries and power-channels between Jesus Christ and the congregation, this is not the case in the New Testament accounts of Jesus' Last Supper, in Paul's discussion of the Supper in 1 Corinthians 10—11, or in John 6 and 13. Indispensable for the celebration of the Lord's Supper are in each case Jesus Christ alone and his flock, rather than ritually ordained clergy. He alone, and not a specific church hierarchy, is to be praised and glorified during this meal.

When the New Testament speaks of the institution of baptism, that is, in the account of Jesus' baptism by John the Baptist, the ministry of powerful proclamation is exercised by the one baptized, not by the baptizer (see esp. Matt. 3:14–15). Similarly, a eucharistic text, (1 Corinthians 11:26), says that all guests at the table of the Lord perform the proclamation of the death of the Lord. All church members who are present, rather than a presiding church officer alone, "do this in remembrance" as joyful celebrants and communal heralds of the crucified, raised, and coming Lord. In short, the New Testament encourages us to understand baptism as the ordination of every Christian and the Lord's Supper as the union, edification, and fortification of the body of Christ in common praise of God, in missionary responsibility, and in brotherly and sisterly love.

For this reason, it is precisely these two sacred acts instituted by Jesus Christ which forbid and make impossible once for all the division of church members into two groups, the clergy and the laity. When BEM says "the ministry was instituted in the revelation accomplished in Christ" (*Min.* 39), it places the divine origin of church offices on the same high level as the unquestionable institution of the sacraments by the Lord. If the authors of BEM had carefully searched for a third partner to form a triad together with baptism and eucharist, then the gospel proclamation, prayer, faithful obedience, mission, or worship in everyday life would have recommended themselves, out of inner necessity and because of their close relationship to baptism and the Lord's Supper. BEM's talk of ministry is a *metabasis eis allo genos*, a change of topic based on preconceived ideas and hidden special interests.

BEM goes so far as to assert that ordained ministers are "representatives" of Christ to the congregation and that in most churches it is the ordained minister presiding at the table of the Lord who demonstrates that the eucharist is a gift of God; the minister is even said to "represent" the divine initiative (*Min.* 11, cf. 12; *Euch.* 29). In consequence, the real presence of Christ at the meal, which is everywhere passionately emphasized, is ascribed not only to the transformed bread and wine but just as much, or even more, to the function and person of the so-called "representative" of Christ ordained through episcopal laying on of hands. But the honor which is thus conferred exclusively on the properly ordained priest really belongs (according to Matt. 25:31–46; 1 Cor. 8; 12; 14; and also in the practice of the ancient church) to the little ones, the weak, and the poor in the congregation.

It is precisely the little ones who count as the most valuable and necessary members of every congregation and of the whole church. A eucharistic celebration that intends to establish communion with the crucified one in any other way than through communion with the least of his brothers and sisters is called by Paul impossible and unworthy; by putting to shame the "have-nots" among the brothers and sisters, it calls down judgment and is therefore catastrophic for the communicants (1 Cor. 11:20–22, 27–33).

Of course, one thing or another could be omitted from or added to the third section of BEM which would modify somewhat the protest which so far has been raised against it, both in this article and in other critical evaluations. For example, the threefold ministry which has been uncritically taken over from Ignatius of Antioch could at least be somewhat relativized by a reference to the fourfold pattern suggested by Calvin. Episcopal succession and the laying on of hands could be mentioned less frequently and less tiresomely as a precondition and sign of the true church and the proper celebration of the sacraments. One could leave a little room for synods and accord them a bit of recognition. The ministry of Peter and the papacy could have been carefully defined, and a few critical remarks concerning its hitherto concrete manifestations could easily have been collected, especially from some recent Roman Catholic scholars.

Why does BEM dodge this issue when de facto the papacy has become an obstacle to unity rather than a symbol of it? However, the real weakness and fundamental wrongheadedness of the BEM statement on ministry are rooted so deeply in the system that one hardly touches them with a few cosmetic changes. In the third part on ministry, BEM brings to light and trumpets to the whole world what was already questionable in parts I and II (baptism and eucharist). Everywhere, to my regret and horror, the notion prevails that a church which relies on its structures and institutions and prides itself on its mandate of sacramental mediation of salvation can unite the presently divided churches and give to the whole world a believable witness to the grace of God.

IV

Do the BEM authors really think that they can contribute to the unity of the churches and a future common expression of faith through the collection, addition, mixture, and compromise of older and newer ecclesiastical traditions?

According to the Preface (paragraph 17), the authors rejoice in the rediscovery of the richness of the common inheritance of all churches. The buried riches which have been discovered and called to our attention consist of ancient and medieval liturgies, doctrines, and traditions, in formulations which stem largely from the First and Second Worlds and which are influenced by their systems of thought and life. What then do they have to say to Third World churches? Instead of ignoring, despising, prejudging, hating, and fighting one another, the authors were prepared to guarantee each other's inherited and well-preserved treasures, while preserving their own possessions. Cooperation and merger instead of competition, a common exterior front instead of mutual internal laceration, the accumulation of capital and the means of production—this is the language used for similar secular endeavors and actions, and it seems that something of the sort also lies behind BEM.

A few examples will illustrate the procedures adopted. In the "epiclesis" of the Eastern churches, the invocation of the Holy Spirit occurs during the consecration, with the conviction that the creator Spirit will change bread and wine into the body and blood of Christ and thus ensure his real presence. In the Western "epiclesis," on the other hand, the Spirit is invoked to sanctify the hearts of believers and to unite dispersed Christians and churches. These two "epicleses" are simply placed side by side in BEM (*Euch.* 14; cf. *Lima Liturgy* 21 and 24), with the result that faith in a physical transformation of the elements is connected amicably and peacefully with a spiritual interpretation of the Lord's Supper. In the East, more weight was put on the Spirit; in the West, on the Word. While the correctly enunciated formula was decisive for the Roman Catholic Church, the Reformation churches emphasized living proclamation, but in both cases the Word was paramount. BEM gives equal weight to both Spirit and Word. Finally, the document suggests the compatibility of the once-for-all sacrifice of Jesus with the concept of a completion and re-presentation of this sacrifice through repeated ecclesiastical acts of sacrifice. On the other hand, a move both bold and overdue has been made when permission is granted in the future to let baptism of children and of "believers" coexist side by side, with equal validity and recognition by all churches.

Since all earthly committees have to find compromises, and since the results of their deliberations are often published in awkward, ambiguous, or simply very poor style, it is no surprise that the present result of almost sixty years' work by the Faith and Order Commission is a compromise document characterized by language which is not only often complicated but almost always less than beautiful. The slang of professional theologians prevails.

More important and surely more offensive, however, is the fact that instead of a search for the one and only truth, which according to John 14:6 is Jesus Christ alone, and to which in their own way all Christian communities once wanted to testify (often with burning zeal and not so rarely even with nasty means), the attempt has been made to compile a series of diverse truths which supposedly can be cheerfully mixed together. The possibility seems not to have been taken seriously that some theological controversies of the past have become unedifying, not to say sterile, because misleading questions had been asked, ugly and queer alternatives were considered crucial, and problematic philosophical premises were elevated to the rank of criteria for describing theological mysteries such as the Lord's Supper.

In BEM, we are confronted with nothing better than an accumulation of incompatible beliefs. Why have we not been presented with the committee's own struggle to find a better understanding of the Bible, to confess one's own and not the fellow Christians' obvious deviations from the gospel, and perhaps even to sing a new song to the Lord concerning baptism and eucharist? The authors might have taken into consideration, for example, a growing consensus among serious recent students of New Testament eucharistic texts, according to which the medieval understanding of the transubstantiation of bread and wine has nothing at all to do with the sense of the biblical wording. Instead of the vapid references to the "ethical implications" of baptism and eucharist, we might have found some strong and clear statements about the failure and the calling of the church in the light of the crying physical and spiritual, communal and personal needs inside and outside the church.

The way BEM is structured and formulated gives the impression of a church that thinks itself rich and sure, faithful and pious. The many references to the Trinity and the corresponding triadic structure of the subsections surely reveal the attempt to engage in centripetal theology and to propose the use of beautiful old liturgies. But it is strange that these references, this structure, and this intention do not lead to the insight and repentance referred to in Revelation 3:17–19: "You say, I am rich . . . not knowing that you are wretched, pitiable, poor, blind, and naked." As if with just a little bit of tolerance and the use of enriched liturgies, a mighty ecumenical advance could be achieved.

Postscript

Among the undeniably important, sometimes even beautiful and clear things one can find in BEM, in spite of its drawbacks, are the frequent references to the divine promises which will be fulfilled only after the end of the present time. BEM's doctrine of the sacraments and ministry, in a word, of the church, differs from a triumphalism pure and simple insofar as it is restrained by the (eschatological) references to the return of Christ, the coming kingdom, and the perfection still to come. And yet the eschatological allusions would have been more convincing if BEM had made very clear (with Eph. 4:13) that the unity of the church, since it lies in God's hands, remains a promise for the future and can certainly not be advanced or produced through the combination of various riches or truths harvested from the past. BEM fails to make it unmistakably clear that the road to unity begins with repentance and that the attainment of the desired goal requires a renewed outpouring of the Holy Spirit, an unrestrained willingness to obey and follow the Lord alone, and the final coming and revelation of Jesus Christ himself. Neither theological nor liturgical manipulation can replace this repentance and openness to Christ and his Spirit.

Because BEM contains an excess of statements that lay claim to an ecclesiastical sacramental mediation of salvation, to an official authority guaranteed by God, and to well-preserved old traditions, I cannot see what use the document might have for inner-church or missionary purposes. As is the case with individual Christians, according to Luther, congregations and churches must also confess that they are themselves beggars. They have contributed and still contribute to the disunity among the churches and among human groups and nations. It is a pity that BEM confirms the churches and their members in the illusion that the solution will come from themselves. It is not clear to me what purpose it serves or what help, what consolation, what faith, and what hope hungry and oppressed people, who live in fear of persecution and war and despair for their very existence, could receive from a document in which the church thinks of itself and presents itself before the whole world as rich, satiated, and secure.

In a speech about BEM, delivered at Temple University in Philadelphia, one of the BEM promoters has stated that its authors expect the following response to their work: the churches are to "receive" the document the way the ancient churches of East and West, North and South "received" the New Testament Canon and the Creeds formulated by the great Ecumenical Councils. Yet even before BEM is received in this or any other way by the churches who contributed to its birth, the Preface of this document announces that it is a beginning and a preview of that statement of faith which Faith and Order will produce in the coming years or decades under the title "Towards the Common Expression of the Apostolic Faith Today." As is said in *Ecumenical Perspectives* (p. 9) with reference to BEM, "That agreement is already a first common expression of the apostolic faith." Is this a reason for joy and confidence? I think it is necessary to pray to God and to request from responsible church authorities that we do *not* proceed in the direction taken so far, but rather return and start once more from the beginning.

This calls for a very qualified "reception"—perhaps following the precedent of many a Parliament or other solemn assembly which "receives" (and sometimes lays aside) a subcommittee report. Since BEM is in its own way a unified, impressive, perhaps classical work, we should refrain from any attempt at picking it to pieces or tinkering with the text. Because neither criticism nor amendment are expected but only an act of reception, the document should in fact be "received" just as it is. It deserves to be thoroughly discussed. But then, with expressions of thanks for services rendered, it should be packed away behind glass and concrete and carefully preserved in a safe place.